We Hold Your Name:

Mormon Women Bless Mormons Facing Exile

Edited by Kalani Tonga and Joanna Brooks

Feminist Mormon Housewives © 2019

We Hold Your Name:
Mormon Women Bless Mormons Facing Exile

Copyright © 2019 Retained by individual authors

All rights reserved.

Cataloging-in-Publication data:

Names: Tonga, Kalani, 1979- editor / Brooks, Joanna, 1971- editor

Title: We Hold Your Name: Mormon Women Bless Mormons Facing Exile / Edited by Kalani Tonga and Joanna Brooks

Cover Design: Tonga, Kalani

Proofreading: Brooks, Joanna / Cannon, Melonie / Denton, Lindsay / Farmer, Mindy May / Hamilton, Raini / Obray, CJ / Rice, Tina Wilberg / Tonga, Kalani

ISBN: 9781797408170

Description: United States: Feminist Mormon Housewives, 2019

For Gina, who would not be silent…

Contents

Kalani's Acknowledgements ~

This was truly a community effort, and as a first-time editor, there are many, many people to thank.

First and foremost, I would like to thank Joanna Brooks for her trust in me and continued mentorship. Thank you for seeing me as I could be, encouraging me to bite off just a little more than I can chew, and then patiently walking with me as I learn from your wisdom and gain confidence in my own abilities. You are Mormon feminism embodied.

Sincere thanks to the behind-the-scenes editing and organizing team: Melonie Cannon, Lindsay Denton, Mindy May Farmer, Raini Hamilton, CJ Obray, and Tina Wilberg Rice. We could never have accomplished a project of this size in such a short time without everyone in this editing team. Thank you for your willingness to work during the busiest season of the year. I know what a sacrifice you made to work during the holidays, and I cannot thank you enough for the gift of your time and talents.

To the Mormon feminist community that continually comes through for sisters in need, thank you for your beautiful contributions to this work. To those who came before and paved the way for those of us who now enjoy the fruits of your labors, we honor your strength and share this work in a spirit of love and sisterhood.

And, finally, to Finau and my little Zoo: thank you for your patience and understanding as I missed making meals and shut myself in my room for hours at a time in order to finish this project. I love you and appreciate you. You are my why.

A note about the cover:

Hongi – the pressing of noses and foreheads – is a Māori custom and is offered in greeting. This intimate gesture shares not only the touch of the seeing eye upon the seeing eye but the breath or hā. Hongi reminds us that we are all one, made from the same substance gifted to us by the Earth-Mother, Papatuānuku. The hongi brings us into relationship with each other and all things. Hongi is a sacred rite of sharing blessing.

Foreword ~

The more time goes on, the more I believe that what gathered the Mormon people--accidental as we are, scattered as we are around the globe--is a shared revolt against death.

We may out of habit start our story with Joseph Smith's "First Vision," his rogue teenage solo encounter with God the Father and Jesus Christ (and in some tellings, God the Mother) in a grove of trees outside Palmyra, New York in 1820. But it is Smith's January 1836 vision of his big brother Alvin--who had died without baptism by immersion or knowledge of Mormonism's "Restored Gospel" and yet had attained full "transcendence" in the highest realms of heaven--that defines us.

What other Western religion has been so audacious as to claim that it can "seal" human relationships--both biological and chosen--against the dissolution and oblivion of death?

After the burial of his friend King Follett in March, 1844, Smith preached, "If you have power to seal on earth & in heaven then we should be crafty . . . go & seal on earth your sons & daughters unto yourself & yourself unto your fathers in eternal glory . . . use a little Craftiness & seal all you can & when you get to heaven tell your father that what you seal on earth should be sealed in heaven."

Why else did so many dislocated, disjointed, displaced, and bereaved peoples give so much to claim a place in the Mormon movement if not to take back their grandmothers and grandfathers, mothers and fathers, sisters and brothers, cousins and kinfolk, from the ravages of modernity?

That's the best I can figure, how my English ancestors wandered out of their ruined forests into the industrial wastes of Manchester and stumbled onto boats and across the American plains in the 1840s, and how the rest of my people, lost in the American South and Southwest since forever, crawled out of the copper mines and cotton fields of Arizona to find Mormonism as well.

To compound the miracle, that's probably why so many indigenous people worldwide, including Maori, chose Mormonism, with its promises of repaired generations and its Book of Mormon-informed positivity towards western indigeneity.

And that's how I met Gina Colvin, the Maori Mormon womanist whose brilliant expositions of Mormonism's colonialist and nationalist blind spots lit up the Mormon bloggernacle and podcasternacle from 2011 onwards. We met first through words, then through Skype, then through the great wandering circuits of global Mormon progressive pilgrimages. And we joined as coordinators and co-authors of *Decolonizing Mormonism* (University of Utah, 2018), a collection of essays contemplating how the Mormon movement has been structured by colonialism and how together we might deconstruct the colonial ideologies privileging white over brown, center over "margin," man over woman, adult over child, heterosexual over all.

But as we know too well, all of us who call ourselves Mormon feminists and womanists, and others besides, Mormonism's absolute confidence in its dominion over death comes at a substantial cost. And we on the faith's progressive margins pay that cost with our lives.

Mormonism's certainty, its conviction of its own sovereignty over death, is predicated on the exclusion – even the expulsion – of those who challenge or question it, even those who do so out of an *extraordinary* and *pressing* love for the Mormon people.

I use the words *extraordinary* and *pressing* intentionally, as our foremother Emma Smith declared at the founding of the LDS Church's[1] Relief Society women's auxiliary, "We are going to do something extraordinary – when a boat is stuck on the rapids with a multitude of Mormons on board we shall consider that a loud call for relief – we expect extraordinary occasions and pressing calls."

And yet many Mormon women who have dared to press extraordinary questions have been informally exiled or formally put to excommunication, a form of social and spiritual death that removes one's

---

[1] The official name of the religious denomination commonly known as the Mormon Church is *The Church of Jesus Christ of Latter-day Saints*, shortened herein to "LDS Church".

name from the records of the LDS Church and from the protection of family relationships sealed for the eternities.

One can only understand or feel how cruel, how violent the threat of exile or excommunication is if one understands that the central and defining impulse of Mormonism is its insistence on non-separation, on unbroken ties that death has no power to sever. We are the ones institutional Mormonism deems expendable, disposable, to satisfy the imperatives of absolute and unchanging LDS rightness.

For the last forty years, Mormon feminists have been living a narrative where the Mormon feminist must die to pay for her challenge to certainty, for her extraordinary and pressing questions and demands, for a reckoning with patriarchy (Sonia Johnson), or with spiritual abuse (Lavina Fielding Anderson), or with the repression of God the Mother (Janice Allred and Margaret Toscano), or with the denial of female priesthood ordination (Kate Kelly). Men have also been subject to excommunication for their extraordinary and pressing questions about Mormon truth claims (John Dehlin) or Mormon racism (George P. Lee).

So, one can imagine our collective sense of terror and grief when we learned in December 2018 that Gina Colvin, whose voice tens of thousands of us took into our innermost selves through her podcast, *A Thoughtful Faith*, as well as her writings and social media posts, had been called to an excommunication court.

And yet, over the last forty years, we had been at work changing ourselves. No longer dependent on institutional narratives of our history and theology, we drew strength from Mormon feminist scholarship and from Mormon feminist organizing that gathered vast communities of affiliation and inquiry. For the first time it became conceivable that no matter the outcome of an LDS Church excommunication court, we might hold each other, as sister members of the Mormon movement, in a Mormon revolt not only against physical death but against the spiritual and social sacrifice that LDS Church excommunication enacts.

We were emboldened certainly by LDS Church leaders' abrupt denunciation of the name "Mormon" in July 2018, their rejection of a treasured gathering point for our shared but peculiar faith situation. We remembered that the Book of Mormon – the ur-text of our movement--

teaches in Mosiah 18 that the prophet Alma fled from the wicked courts of power to gather the faithful on the "borders" or margins of the land, *at the waters of Mormon*, and there committed them to hold each other, to share each other's sorrows and burdens, and to be one people.

We realized that so long as we held each other's names, so long as we shared each other's sorrow and burdens, we could belong to each other still as Mormons.

And somehow death might lose its sting, and the grave of spiritual expulsion its victory (1 Corinthians 15:55).

We took fresh courage too in remembering--first through scholarship and then through quiet but determined feminist action on the faith's margins-- that Mormon women had from the beginnings of our movement claimed the power to bless each other, to lay hands on each other and pronounce (through faith or through priesthood as endowed in LDS temple ceremonies) blessings upon each other's lives. We had pulled language cues from archival fragments, and with apologies to our forebears and ancestors, we reconstructed some sense of how to bless each other. And we practiced, at Mormon feminist retreats in mountain cabins, in empty hotel conference rooms in Salt Lake City, in the upper rooms of bookstores in Provo, Utah, under the cottonwood trees at Mormon feminist summer camp in Hobble Creek Canyon, and via Skype and Facebook messenger calls spanning languages, nations, and continents.

We learned how to hold, bless, and keep each other as a Mormon people against whatever institutional expulsion or death the LDS Church might enact.

This book is a collection of Mormon women's blessings for Mormons facing exile, generated by more than eighty Mormon women – from literary legends like Carol Lynn Pearson and prize-winning poets like Susan Howe to dozens of emerging or first-time writers – as Gina Colvin's December 2018 excommunication court loomed. Gina envisioned this book first, not for herself, but for all Mormon people facing exile because they too asked *extraordinary* and *pressing* questions, or simply lived the truths of their bodies and hearts.

In these pages you will find expressions of Mormon feeling as wide and divergent as this many-branched movement, and they are all here for you, gathered, to be recounted in those moments when you feel you do not fit in LDS institutional life, to assure you that no one and nothing can eradicate your belonging to Mormonism so long as you wish to identify with it.

We hold your name. That is our promise, to each other, on the margins, in twenty-first century Mormonism. We claim you among those willing to take on a rejected identity, to share each other's sorrows and burdens, and to stand firm against the idea that any one of us is expendable to sacrifice or expulsion.

Whether you are a classic Mormon feminist visionary rebel in the proud tradition of Sonia Johnson and Kate Kelly, or a wounded but loving theological healer in the mold of Margaret Toscano and Janice Allred, or an LGBTQIA2S Mormon moving into your truth, or an indigenous Mormon or Mormon of color grappling with the institution's shortcomings and betrayals, or simply someone living in a conservative LDS ward that refuses to see your beauty and your authenticity, may these blessings name, claim, comfort, and hold you, in the beauty and power of our ever-dynamic and rebellious Mormon movement, in the name of the Mother, and the Father, and all who came before us. Amen.

Joanna Brooks, December 2018

Poems and Blessings ~

Alisa Bolander ~

She was born into the struggle
Between ego and creation
And under the fear of others
She learned to ask for permission
She learned who she may call her friends
Learned that her body must belong to them

Born of a mother, wrenched open and torn,
Swearing, sweating, panting and praying
With swelling cyclones in her breast
Pulling with desire to nurture and save

Men saw her mother grow ripe and full-round in the belly
Heard her joy-screams and saw how miraculously she split in two
How life rushed through her and bloomed out of her
She tore open to bring our world into being
And yet lived

And they were terrified
Not for her sake,
Not because the birth was red and shadowy
Slippery, the stuff of death
Terrified that she became two, then three, then more
That she created and saved with everything she had in her body
Poured her mind into jars, into pitchers, down the waterfalls
Placed all her song into the roots of trees
Where they fed each green leaf pointed toward the sun
That her hair was a curtain of water lilies
And her steps healed up every tear
And she still lived
They knew they couldn't put a stop to it

So they raided the jar
Called her profane and dammed her rivers
Behind shut doors, in booming echoes
Formed councils and priesthoods
With locked shoulders and full-weighted hands

1

They blocked her way
Taught her daughter to sing their songs

We will give you life, they said
Obey.
Our bread shred in pieces
This is our labor
It is all for you
You were born in us
You will rip yourself in two
You will shed your blood in return for spilling water

She tried to make a life inside their glass cases
A good daughter
This construction could not hold
At first, it chipped, it streaked and cracked
It snapped and twisted at 90 degrees
The glue turned old and crumbled
The iron rusted away
Leaving only everything as she was, In flesh and in mind

Worlds she made in her head and in her body
Screaming forth from her engine heart
Intelligence pulsing from her pupils
Irises of light
Her creation-song
Blowing through curtains and flowing between veils
Under dams and in every crack
Diffusing the atmosphere
Nourishing the bed of earth

I belong here
I belong to myself
I cannot be moved from myself
Born with the universe spinning in my heart

Amanda Farr ~

The other day, in what would be *my* darkest pain,
Should our situations be reversed:
You asked.

You asked about my person.
You ask to meet her.
You asked to understand.
You asked to know.
You asked to experience.
My joy.

In moments that might crush others: You asked.

The other day, when so much was happening,
When others might be distracted,
You shared.

You shared about abstaining from alcohol.
You shared about your life.
Shared your experience.
Shared your successes.
Shared your failures.

In something that felt trivial:
You shared.

The other day, feeling the wind that has yet to reach my face, halfway
around the world:
You carried on.
You spoke your truth when others wished you silent.
Spoke of truth.
Spoke of yearning.
Spoke of commitment and faith and trust.

There are men who want to stop you.

No more asking.
No more sharing.

3

No more speaking.

There are women, women who have gone before who have stopped.

I do not know their names.

When the wind touches my face, I do not know which women it has touched.

But I know you.
I know your name.
I know you were not created in the image of the divine in order to stop.

Ask. Share. Speak.

Send the wind my way.

Amy Caston ~

I heard a voice
crying in the wilderness,
calling out from atop a city wall--
a voice I heard with my ears,
read with my eyes,
felt in my soul.
Would God send this stranger
to me,
to speak Truth?
God, who knows me
and draws me toward
light
understanding
growth

I heard her voice
and I wandered into the wilderness to hear;
I looked up to see
and felt my heart opening.
This stranger,
my sister,
bringing the voice of God to me:
light
growth
understanding

We heard her voice--
in the brilliance, we see ourselves.
To understand, we must break open
what we were
and grow into more.

They heard her voice;
why do they decry it?
They do not want to hear
God's voice,
not from her,
this stranger.

5

They think to silence her.
I fear, thinking
she is alone in the wilderness,
unprotected atop the wall.
What can I do?

I watch, sorrowing,
as they ready their arrows.
I cry out to God--
our God,
God of the strangers,
God of my sisters,
God of light.
I witness:
their arrows cannot touch her.

It is God's voice in her.

Amy Rich ~

To our newest matron saint - we honor you.

Like Maya and Malala, your words fight your battles for truth and higher purpose.

Like Frida and Amelia, you ignore gender barriers thrown at you and break those barriers down with your grace and genius.

Like so many women, you do the work, time and time again, and continue to push against a broken system that says "no vacancy" for strong feminist voices.

Like me, you want to rest knowing that your efforts will reap a time in the near future where equality, honesty and respect are given out freely to all who have breath.

Like a divine goddess, you see the bigger picture and choose to live your higher truth, regardless of the little ant men in suits and ties who crawl around pretending to be important to the colony.

You are Wisdom
You are Courage
You are Truth
You are Queen

You are Free

Annalicia Whittaker ~ A Faith Transition, or what it means to be Strong ~

You know when your soul shifts?
an infinitesimal shift,
and when you look back –
two inches has become Gondwanaland and Laurasia.

Suddenly the pew isn't soft anymore and
The friendly hand-shakes hide something more sinister

when were you ever there?
and how did you get here?

The callings, the baptisms, the blessings,
The weak to be visited and cajoled into activity,
It <u>was</u> the *weak* who didn't have the strength to stay –

But today is different,

Oh ye of little faith doesn't mean "them" anymore.
It might mean you.

So what is strength? And who decides?

STRENGTH: a mother who thought you important enough to include in
the women's bitching circle, the same mother who asked if you wanted a
period-party to celebrate the vaginal-blood-ritual that signifies your move
from pubescent primary into a horrified almost-adult.

STRENGTH: The women who rewrote the ends to their own fairy-tales,
the beloved child's hymn, the joyous dissonance of opera's "traditional"
pants roles.

STRENGTH: the resurrected voices of Joan of Arc, Lucy Stone, Eliza R
Snow, and the unpublished prophetesses.

STRENGTH: replacing Gods' masculine pronoun with a plural one, and
marching in a parade that four years ago would have meant
excommunication.

– This shift means you no longer fit.

You are a "them" – the feminists and weaklings and questioners and doubters and all the hosts of the tower of Babylon that you were warned about.

Whether you identify as such is irrelevant,

So –
Is Strength having the courage to stay, or to walk away?

Ariel Wootan Merkling ~

I used to think that blessings were like a genie in a lamp
Laying on of hands
A spoken wish
And a miracle

But now I know that blessings are a circle of light
drawn around those we love
Full of mystery and grace
To carry with us on the journey
Rather than a shortcut to the happy ending

And so I offer you a blessing

The blessing of Eve
As you leave the garden
May your grief deepen compassion
May the new vistas fill you with holy excitement

The blessing of Sariah
A prophetic voice in the wilderness
The blessing of courage to speak hard words
May you find hope and joy in the wilderness
May your voice never waver

The blessing of the mothers of the sons of Helaman
Whose refusal to return violence brought a community to repentance
As you follow the path of peace
May we put down our weapons of spiritual warfare and repent

The blessing of Abish
Whose stretched out hand awoke the sleeping
May we at your touch awake from apathy, fear, systems of oppression
and violence
And sing the songs of redeeming love

The blessings of the Mormon mothers
Who show up with homemade bread and handmade quilts
May you feel loved and supported
Carried and protected
May we anticipate your needs and provide respite for your heart.

Ashmae Hoiland ~ Down the Hill ~

When Jutta died, Hildegard of Bingen was made a leader of the nuns.
She didn't want to remain in the stone complex issued them. She wanted
to take her
group and move into their own space, a move
towards temporary poverty. And sovereignty.

The first man in charge would not allow her independence.
So she went to higher authority and got approval.

I remember so clearly the demarcation I sensed when I brought my idea
for missionary work to the bishop's meeting. "Yes!" he said. "That's
wonderful!" and then proceeded to repeat what we would do. It wasn't
my idea any more, but my idea twisted into his, carried out in his way,
until my contribution was unrecognizable. I grabbed my anger, lest it be
colonized,
and stuffed it back down my throat before nodding
at the close of the prayer and leaving the room.

A sickness struck Hildegard that left her paralyzed when again she was
denied.

Defiance laced with feigned ineptitude is something every woman could
probably hearken back to. Sometimes it's the only way to get things
done.

The Abbot himself could not move Hildegard from her bed, and in this
realization, he relented and Hildegard rose, twenty women following her
down the hill to their new home.

Sometimes being a feminist means proclaiming loudly what is yours, and
sometimes it is simply getting up and walking away.

Blaire Ostler ~ We Were Rebuked ~

They told us be like your Father who art in heaven.
They told us follow the example of your brother Jesus.
They told us be made perfect in Him.
They told us we are made in His image.
They told us listen to the Spirit, He will confirm the truth.
They told us come follow me, so we did.

Yet, we were rebuked.

We were rebuked for following His example.
We were rebuked for believing we are made in His image.
We were rebuked for calling on His priesthood power.
We were rebuked for claiming our divine nature.
We were rebuked for believing all are alike unto God.
We were rebuked for believing the Spirit confirmed truth.

Who knew obedience to the patriarchs
was a punishable offense?

Mother, forgive them,
for they know not what they do.

Brittany Romanello ~

In the cold white office, with carpet on the walls
He asks me in front of strange men
What made my legs open wide.
Will I still belong if I am not sad I did it?
What should I ask him in return?
I sit and I think:
What makes a lover?
What makes a slut?
I was groomed for this.
You don't think it's true?
Mmmmm, Repressed girls
Grown men growl at me with
A wink and smile.
Laughing because they know
They'll get what they want from me later.
I'll give it freely. I like to submit.
I like pain. I like it so much I ask for it.
I choke. I'm accustomed to it.
Other women like me know why.
For years we swallowed this:
The message-You are less.
You are of man, but not of his stature.
Your purpose is to serve him.
Serve God, serve your father, serve your husband.
Serve the men, and pray for sons.
Birth the men, love the men, idolize the men,
Cradle them to your virtuous breasts.
Cook for them, clean for them
Let them preside over you in righteousness.
Answer to them
Find beauty in your role. Be beautiful, stay beautiful.
Stay thin, stay small, stay tight.
Give them your whole soul. Do this without complaint.
Find glory in your duty, it has been sanctified for you!
Suits and ties were the uniform for God's love,
And God's love is conditional.
You must listen. You must fear the not listening.
You must cover your knees. Your shoulders. Your laughter.

14

Is this not the covenant?
You must tacitly know how to please a man
Without him ever having touched your naked flesh.
You must give pleasure without knowing
What it feels like within yourself.
Wait. Do you touch yourself? No! No!
Good girls don't. Don't be bad, baby.
Am I sexual?
Am I coy?
Am I mysterious?
Am I easy?
Am I dirty?
Am I desirable?
Am I turning you on?
I prayed for this. Yes, I was an accomplice.
This was prayed for, for me - in temples and at altars
That I could become this woman.
The one that adores you.
The one that entertains you.
The one that cries with you, and for you.
The one the community can be proud they raised.
The one who brings honor to her parents.
Mom and Dad, I wish for you to feel honored.
Do you feel honored by me?
I am a pliable woman. A virtuous woman. A ruby-
Precious above gold. Who am I?
An obedient woman.
Obedient women-
They will compromise self-preservation for your self-indulgences.
She is a supple virgin bride, lift her up and open wide.
Yes, I am the perfect woman.
I am attainable, achievable, conquerable.
I think not of myself. How could I?
And always, I think of the most Holy and most High.
Can you understand?
I opened my flower to him. Is that not my salvation?

I am sweet. I am ripe. I am Eve.
I am the fruit, I am the knowledge, and the serpent too.
It seems when they ask why I did it, they don't understand.
Yes, strange as it may be, it's very clear
The same things that make a slut, they also make a saint.

Callie Ngaluafe ~

Wildness.
(Strangeness.)

Night.

The untamed hair,
the undiluted stars.

She walks with the moon,
and she is
                free--

Climbing the green mountains
that brush against the last
                        forever--

Beyond anything you could guess or apprehend.

Her heart yearns and yearns
and will not be satisfied.

The lake at midnight--
the slate, cold water
in rivulets runs on her skin,
drips from her hair

and wildness flares--

like a star hurtling
toward her earth.

It lives, it grows, it pounds
at your door--

It lashes and bites and
cannot be doused
by your careful, correct, bloodless
pronouncements.

17

Carol Lynn Pearson ~ Haiku for Gina ~

My name written on
the palm of God's hand never
can be blotted out.

Cheryl Bruno ~ Hymn to the Woman-God ~

Praise to the woman-God
who applauds the efforts and crayon-sketches of her children
and requires not offerings of guilt.

Honor the woman-God
who will have them kiss and make up when angry with their siblings
and buries all weapons in the bottom of the toy-box.

Worship the woman-God,
who sends not down her children to the abyss
for their passions, crimes and thoughts.

Her form is a shapely one
whose breasts leak on occasion, hearing their cries
so she gathers, hides, and saves.

Cheryl Bruno ~ A Toast ~

The table where I grew up
eating breakfast and lunch and Thanksgiving dinner
was always large enough
for one more.

We put the babies on laps
and bumped elbows--
no "kids' table" allowed.
If you came late and there wasn't space,
we'd pull up another table,
flush against the other,
Added upon.

We held hands and sang our prayers
and everyone took a deep
breath before the final "Amen,"
So we could hold out the harmony
forever and ever
floating it up to the skies
where I imagined the angels joined in.

I pictured tables like ours
in the celestial spheres--
always another to pull up,
winding around in a serpentine chain,
crooked and caddy-wompus with mismatched tablecloths.

So when my Church said
there was no room at the table
for you--
You! The one who always
washed your hands and set the silverware and
shared the very last piece of pie,

I stopped what I was doing,
And clinked my glass
until I was joined by
a large number of other unruly noisemakers

and raised my glass
in a salute
and a toast to your honor:

Let angels and these witnesses
join us at the Heavenly Table
where, somehow
God sits next to each one of us.

Christa Baxter ~

What weight can words carry?
How could they lessen the spiritual violence
of men gathered in a room
discussing your eternal fate?

(The hubris of it would be laughable
were it not so painful to think of.)

Still, I'll wrap what words together I may
I'll tell you the ways you've changed the world
With words upon words upon words.

You taught me the utility of anger.
I, an American Mormon girl of pioneer descent,
had been taught to fear anger all my life.
And you carried it without fear.

You, and women like you,
Reminded me that anger is a gift
A reminder that we are worth being angry for
That a heart honest to life's pain
Can be open to its joy.

And you probably don't remember the summer night
You leaned in close and told me
With such frankness and clarity
"If he can't honor the gift that is your body
then leave."

Can I ever convey what a blessing that was?

You have stood in circles with me
On cool August evenings in the mountains
Laying hands upon woman after woman
Calling down strength, calling her into community.

With the light of the July sun
Streaming through stained glass
I've heard your voice soar and soar
Proclaiming belief in Christ
Redeeming the memory of your mother
Offering grace to the wounded

And as we approached, one by one
To take the eucharist and stand before you
Your finger traced the cross upon our foreheads
And you pronounced us blessed.

My heart leapt and wept to have a woman
Claim her spiritual gifts
And use her power to bless.

And these days when I pray,
I hear your words in my mind
"Mother Father God"
The only greeting the makes any sense to me now.

In the face of all you have given me
I suppose I can't say that words
Are a small matter, after all.

It must be acknowledged:
Some men will gather soon enough
And their words will come to pass
And then pass away

Meanwhile, we walk forward
Meanwhile, we hold our arms wide for you
Bolstered by an anger that dared us to love ourselves
Wholly, completely, unafraid
Meanwhile, we will weave these words
Into a web of stars
Reflecting back the love and the courage
The fury and the wit
The unafraid, belly-deep laughter
That has run through all your words.

We carry you forward
Sharing you through your words
All of us, doing what we can
To weave a world with more love and less fear.

CJ Obray ~ Diagramming Sentences ~

For Gina, and all the rest.

Light and knowledge
cannot be extinguished
by a puff of passing wind.

Integrity
cannot be doused
by a random drop of water.

Eternal ties
cannot be severed
by bureaucratic scalpels.

Prophetic voices
cannot be silenced
by cacophony
from the Sanhedrin.

What *would* Jesus do?

Embrace the questioner;
love the injured;
rebuke the bully;
denounce those
who would wield authority
as a weapon.

Court of love, indeed.

Truth shines
no less brightly
though blocked from view.

Angels will sing,
should we listen or not.

Truth speaks truth to Power.
Angels *will* sing.
Shepherds will *hear*.

CJ Schneider ~

May Mother Eve step forward from the world of our ancestors
to put her arm around you and say
"I've been banished before too you know
...and darling...
that was the beginning of everything."

Cynthia Bailey Lee ~

We met by joining our voices
Together, One voice,
In the same joyful song.
I still believe All God's creatures got a place in the choir.
I still sing with you.

Danna Myers Hook ~ Remember ~

Remember the warmth and the love when you were eight.
Remember the feeling of following Christ as you entered the waters of
baptism. You remember.
God remembers.
No man can take that.
Ever.
Remember the excitement of joining your life with another.
Remember the holiness of kneeling across the altar to make promises.
You remember.
The Divine remembers.
No man can take that.
Ever.
Remember the conflict and fear when troubles came.
Remember the peace and courage when your sisters gathered round. I am
here.
Goddess is here.
No man can take that.
Ever.

Dayna Patterson-Kidd ~ Post-Mormons Are Leaving ~

Post-Mormons are leaving the circled-up pioneer wagons for wide open plains.

Post-Mormons are leaving, crushed under ox-pulled wagon wheels, their jaws broken, lungs punctured.

They bear heavy family trees on their shoulders, the weight of eight generations, roots raking the earth. They carry their children's children on their shoulders, packs and handcarts filled with susurrate rust.

Post-Mormons are the new Ex-Mormons. Or rather, Post-Mormons are Ex-Mormons who've swallowed embers and live to say, *That was me.*

Ex-Mormons see shards. Post-Mormons see a new bottle, the old bottle standing by, other bottles near: glass flasks, liquor cylinders, spirits bottles. Some tapered. Some ribbed. Some squat and square.

Post, Latin for *after / behind*

Ex, Latin for *out of*

Post-Mormons, then, are the ticker tape *after* the parade, fallen and trampled, swept together for recycling.

Ex-Mormons, then, are fugitives fleeing *out of,* refugees from the bombed city, survivors of the kill zone, escapees.

Post-Mormons are leaving the harsh x (like hex) of the Ex-Mormons and gathering their sorrow into the O of Post.

Post-Mormons are leaving the walled garden's knowledge tree with its satisfying fruit to scavenge glacial soil's mysterious sustenance.

They are leaving in droves, hemorrhaging from wards and stakes and missions around the world.

They aren't leaving because they want to get intimate with evil or because someone swapped their cream for 1%.

29

They're leaving because conscience needles. Because better angels prick. Because the path where they find their feet nettles, tricked with weeds.

They're leaving bible bags. Missionary name tags. A stack of seminary manuals.

Post-Mormons hold an expired temple card. They remove their magic underwear, the magic gone, roll them and stack them like cords of white firewood, stow them in closets. Or shred them for cleaning cloths. Or burn them in a backyard bonfire.

Mine in a bedside bin. My husband's in the garage, boxed up.

Post-Mormons are teens in grownup bodies. They purple their hair. They ink their skin. They pierce noses and tongues and navels.

They are alcohol virgins. They hold a salt-rimmed margarita. A chilled sangria. A champagne flute.

They are coffee virgins. They drink their first latte. First iced cappuccino. First mocha with whip.

They are smoke virgins. Some puff their first cigarette. First cigar. First joint.

Their *Thou shalt nots* turn to *Why nots* or *Maybe nots* or *I'd rather nots*.

Some leave husband or wife and kids. Attempt open marriage. Come out.

My mother and her wife, married at the end of a long December.

Post-Mormons walk barefoot over the wreckage of faith crisis, exchange bleeding digits for free time. They take up cycling and watercolor. They take up fly fishing and poetry. They take up bartending and competitive Scrabble.

On Sunday, they hike or shop or sleep or clean house.

Sometimes they miss getting all dressed up and sitting snug in a family pew and singing congregational hymns and carols. The chapel's sanctuary a down quilt of quiet.

But those crazy angels with their hot pokers.

Post-Mormons are leaving in the night, trailing red across a frozen river.

Post-Mormons are leaving, a quail flock following not far behind.

Post-Mormons are leaving, a pocketful of sunflower seeds to scatter as they go.

Dovie Onice Eagar Peterson ~

may you
your kindred
familial and found
be upheld
traipsing siblings
in this travail

with our prayers
may we hold up
your arms
until the sun
goes down

the spiral compass
in my chest
inclines towards you

your words have been
a lower light
aligned with
The Light
marking safe passage
to the shore
for me

may you navigate
present stormy seas
trusting in
JESUS
at this crossing
to safe harbor

Emily Summerhays ~

There's a pain at the core of me
that bears no name.
Swaddled in silence
anointed with tears
I forbade
from coursing down my cheeks.
Wrapped in bravado
sealed with laughter
I share with my sisters
at the folly of men.

There is much to laugh about.

And cry about.
And seethe about.
It never ends.
One eternal round.
(What fresh hell is this?)

The righteous indignation has long since
burnt out.
The fury
I didn't bother expressing
(he who has ears let him hear)
collapsed
on itself
like a dying
star
shining brightly
for the whole world to see
but they wouldn't
Look.
Let alone Listen.

Leaving a dark little pearl,
never cast before swine.
No woman can serve two masters.
For they will both tell her to destroy herself.

Fuck that noise.
We bless ourselves instead.

It's hard,
and it hurt
as I walked
and walked
and walked
and walked
leaving Eden behind me
with its flaming swords
but now
its burden is light.
See?

Sisters.
Let us go
take our pearls
and string
together
a necklace.
One eternal round
Gracing the throats of the
daughters
of Zion
who were told
they could never come home.

For shining too brightly.
For the whole world to see.

Let us go.
Tears
laughter
fury
voices
rising upward
toward heaven.
Let us go.
Let us go.

Esther Dale ~

Gina.
Beloved of Heaven.
I bless you with the love of one sister to another.
I lift my voice to ask Heaven to protect your spirit
As you speak with the voice and inspiration given you by God.
They who fear your voice and words of truth seek to silence you
But they cannot.
I lift my hands to ask Heaven to guide your steps
As you walk in the power given you by God,
Power that men envy,
But they cannot take it from you.
May you always walk in the knowledge of the presence of Our Mother,
Secure in the knowledge of Her Love for you.
Bless you.

Fatimah Salleh ~

Mother of All,
Hold on to us, your daughters, when the world tries to snatch us from your embrace.
Come for us when we're travailing the violence set to submerge us.
Remind me I am yours and nothing can separate me from your love.
Whisper again my innate goodness, my unyielding connection to You.
Look for me when I seem lost and remind me I've always been found.
With my tears of my testimony, clear a healing path for me and my sisters.
In the name of the One who holds us All.
Amen.

Gretchen Walker ~

Dear Gina, a sweet sister whose strength I have drawn from, I want to say
thank you.
Thank you for helping me see that religion does not equal spirituality.
Thank you for taking God out of a box. You helped me to see God
everywhere, which means everything to me.
Thank you for shining your light even though others would have it be
dimmed. Your "mess" is beautiful, and I would bless that you and your
family find joy together in that.
You helped guide me through my first women's blessing, which was
earth shattering and heart healing and brought me to where my soul and
true self is. Thank you.
Thank you for putting into words all that has been stuck inside me for a
long time.
This letter says a lot about me, but I know you have influenced and
changed so many people across the world. Your strength is beautiful.
Your weaknesses are beautiful. Thank you for sharing both of them.
Love,
Gretchen Walker

(*God, Faith, Women & Church: SLC April 2017*)

Heather Harris-Bergevin ~ Bridle All Your ~

We, too, have traveled
this path. They attempted
to place upon us, also,
the scold's bridle, used
when a woman thinktalks too
freely for their liking, these town
Elders. I've been led to the square, had
the bit placed in my mouth, hands
bound, led around to jeers. They mean to silence
womanthought, some men, and the others
stand confused, thinking the elders must
have misunderstood your words. They did not.
This gentle violence, they say, is carved
from love... they say. Women must not
speak in the church, they read to us.
Paul was divine, and he should know. So, keep
your hair covered, keep your head down, they say,
Submit
to your punishment. It will be over
soon enough. But, it is never over, the feel of the
iron cage around your head, metal tang upon
your tongue. The men might look
on you as one branded with the mark
of a scold, but we, the women, will not,
because, in all, there are but few
of us left who have not worn the bridle,
meant to curb our tongues, our passions,
our thinking, our action, and those
who have not worn it, yet,
give it time. Eventually all women
are to be scolded.

Heather Holland ~ May We All Be ~
For Gina

If it is a sin
to seek God in all her glory,
God as wide as wind-swept prairies,
high as a sharp-shinned hawk
that rides a circlet of wind
over red cliffs shaped by millennia
of wind and water—

If it is a sin
to find God in his deliciousness and delight,
the God of joy and opening
who welcomes all the strangers in
saying: Come! Come!
Share a square of chocolate
and a glass of deep red with me!
We shall hold hands and laugh together,
play the ukulele and sing in tumbling harmony—

If it is a sin
to share with your brothers and sisters
a God big enough to hear our sorrows
as we rail against gods made in the image
of men in red power ties, to whisper
to those hurting around the globe:
It is okay to cry, to grieve,
but hush, hush, my dear ones.
Do not be afraid to lose the gods
who cannot bear your doubts,
your soft tears, your choking cries in the night—

If this is sin, may we all be sinners.

If this is worthy of excommunication,
may we all be thrown out on our ears
to stand and look each other in the eyes

and grin our madness as we see
how gently we are held by a God more vast
than they have ever imagined,
than we will ever imagine.

Jami Kimball Baayd ~

Land in Casablanca
Drive eight hours south
Through switchbacks
Over mountains
And dirt roads
Until you find a small oasis
At the edge of the desert

Park near the mosque
Ask the first woman you find
"Hamam afeck?"
She will take you by the hand
Guide you
Through the tunnels between adobe houses
To the door of hamam

Leave your clothes in the front room
Take the ball of brown soap she offers
Say bsimillah — in God's name — when you enter the inner room

Sit by the woman who beckons to you
If you like, she will wash your hair
Your body
With that soft brown soap
They will tell jokes in a language you don't understand
The sound bouncing around the stone walls
They will scrub your skin until it shines
Carrying buckets of warm water
To bathe you

This is the holiest place I can offer you
Here you are safe in woman's sacred touch

Jen Perlmutter Tanner ~ At One Ment ~

What if Christ's atonement
never really was about
a bloodthirsty God's need
for a human sacrifice?

What if all along
Jesus knew
that the punishment for
speaking out
and standing up
against the oppression
the hypocrisy
and the cruelty
by the religious elite
was death by crucifixion?

What if he ministered to
the outcasts
anyway?
What if he brought
hope
and healing
to the hurting
and the vulnerable
anyway?

What if each act of
speaking truth to power
and each act of courage
in standing up to
the rulers
on behalf of
the marginalized
was his truest teaching
of what it really
means to be
at one
with Him?

I'm trying to be like Jesus.
I'm following in His ways.
It feels revolutionary
and terrifying
and freeing,
but what if
He understands?

What if
as we walk
this challenging path,
we're becoming more
at one
with Him
than ever before?

Jen Perlmutter Tanner ~ **A Blessing** ~

You've shared communion
with broken bread, crackers
and Diet Coke.
You've created sacred
from the mundane
and blessed my forehead.
You've listened
and named the needs,
and done it all with love.

Now I bless you
through prayers,
lighted candles,
and my heart lifted up
with yours
Strengthening you
and reminding you
that you aren't alone
in any of this.

I bless you with a reminder of
the Goddess
who is too often forgotten
and silenced
by patriarchy.

She lives in you.
She encircles you,
as we all do now.
May She continue to
remind you of
the Goddess
you already are,
and pour out
an endless supply
of blessings
upon your life.

Jenna Colvin ~

Men in collared shirts and ties
Speak on behalf of God.
They tell me what He thinks,
What He wants me to do.

But in quiet, sacred moments,
Alone
I reach for God
And feel Her near.

Collared shirts and ties
Can't stand between me and my mother.

Jennifer Gonzalez ~

The futility of it all

Silencing a voice
that has already spoken,
as if the reverberating echoes
can be pulled back
from the canyon walls.

Plucking out
that which offends,
but it is the body that bleeds
and bleeds
and bleeds
and bleeds,
weakening the flesh
beyond the ability to fight back
against the festering, marbled necrosis.

The presumption of authority
pales in the face of actual power.

Jo Overton *(Sicangu Lakota)* ~

In the darkness, the tears come
Broken heart, love betrayed
Lies disguised as promises
Whitewashed hatred unleashed
Her head bowed in sorrow

She lifts her chin, resolute
Her eyes fill with Heaven's lights
Angels singing for her
Proud and true
Our hearts intertwined in love
Poet, prophetess, goddess gift
You are not alone
We stand with you
 I am just one of many

Jody England Hansen ~

At this time when so many names are spoken in vain,
When the name Mormon, the place which was precious and joyful to
those who shouted out,
"Yes! I will share burdens to lighten them.
I will live the one-ness that God leads me to be!"
When this beautiful name Mormon is linked to evil, and is excised
because of man's vanity…
When the name of Christ is used as a weapon to tear asunder,
When the name apostate is used to justify fear and violent abuse,
I will turn away from the vain speaking.

At this time of remembering Mary,
the woman who embraced the power of birthing God into the world,
Mary, the expression of the Goddess who invited us all into wisdom,
called us all forward to have space within us to grow into new life,
this Mary, who was not the ideal,
with no authority or position,
who was at risk of death because of men who turned to lettered rules first,
and inspired love last.
Mary, who chose to journey into unknown possibility,
And to Elizabeth.

At this time when I remember Elizabeth hurrying to embrace Mary,
Exclaiming, "The god in me sees the god in you. I rejoice with you!"
No shaming, only sharing creation, and blessings.

At this time when we are so hungry for the good news,
Yet we are always holding each other in the wound,
Distance cannot stop my trying to reach out,
In offering, in blessing, in comfort, love, peace.
I would… for you.
I would break open the vessel.
I would pour all of the precious oil,
Declaring you divine.
We are all the anointed,
Anointed by the blessed oil,
by the blood of the wound,
by the blood of death, and of new birth.

48

Bless you with all you require as you create the life of God in the world,
In all the tribes you claim and grace,
Woman, Maori, Mormon, Christian, Ordained, abundant endless body of
Christ,
Whole and holy,
As you move beyond the vanity and idolatry of men,
Bless you, that you may be held by God, who is with you in this wound.

At this time, the god in me sees the god in you,
Weeping in the wound, and rejoicing in creation.
I am with you.

Judith Curtis ~ Being Born a Woman and a Saint ~

I am a woman born, of all rights shorn,
Assured by men it is God's will. I mourn
Their wanton inability to see
That we all have equal share in Christ's bounty.
To home and hearth my fate is relegated
Until their great desire for power is sated
And women, freed at last from Eden's curse
Will return to glory, blessed, as we were at first.

Kalani Tonga ~ Mixed Blessings ~

Nobody told me when I set out to find God for myself
The burning in my bosom might consume my church home.

I didn't know when I dug for doctrinal answers
I'd bury the religion of my birth, but uncover the treasure that is my
spirituality.

Nothing prepared me to look my temple-loving sisters in the face
And tell them I felt assaulted in the place they'd found peace.

As I looked for a God who looked like me,
I didn't expect to see Her in the women the prophets called
dangerous and labeled apostates.

I don't think we ever quite get over
The unexpected rejection of a community
we thought was the body of Christ.

But, if the body of Christ lacks eyes to see the vulnerable,
If it lacks ears to hear the voices speaking truth to power,

Then maybe this is not the whole body, but merely an appendage
of a body not yet fully grown.

I didn't anticipate outgrowing the Mormon church,
But the church has outgrown its own Mormon-ness,
so maybe growth just looks like rejection around here.

I'm sorry, friend, that they can't see us for who and what we are.
I'm sorry they see weeds where we plant strength,
And they see threats where we speak truth and love.

I mourn with you the loss of what was.
I sit with you in the fear and sadness and anger of what is.
I celebrate with you the freedom of what will be.

You are loved.
You are enough.

Kate Kelly ~ Fuck the Patriarchy, A Poem ~

F
u
c
k

t
h
e

p
a
t
r
i
a
r
c
h
y.

Amen.

Kathryn Elizabeth Shields ~ A Name and a Blessing ~

O Woman,
Having been given no authority,
Neither from on high or by man,
I give you a name and a blessing.
The name by which you shall be known
In the rolls kept in the broken hearts of your sisters
Is Courage.
This name has always existed in you,
And it cannot be taken from you.

I bless you that if your people turn you away,
You may find strength in yourself.
I bless you that Peace will come to you and
Wrap you in her embrace.
May you listen to your spirit and feed her well.
The universe knows and loves you.
It is better for your being here.
We are all better for your being here,
For your voice.
No group of men,
Claiming authority and inspiration from God,
Can ever take away your access to heaven,
Because salvation
Is already stitched into your being.

Katie Langston ~ A Prayer ~

God of reconciliation,
Sometimes it's impossible to imagine that there can be anything but violence.
We hurt others, and they hurt us.
We draw sharp lines.
We draw swords.
But you have promised a path through vengeance:
Mercy, self-giving, grace.
We are incapable of doing it on our own.
Help us, change us, save us.
Lord in your mercy,
Hear our prayer.

God of healing,
We Mormons are a broken people.
Our history is full of coercion and fear.
We have lied to each other.
We have lied to ourselves.
We have lied to you.
Help us to face what is real.
Remind us that no truth is so terrible that it's better to stay in denial.
Help us repent:
Of idolatry, of injustice.
Bring judgment, then mercy, then wholeness.
Lord in your mercy,
Hear our prayer.

God of wisdom,
Gina has been blessed with gifts of insight, clarity, and grace.
Sustain her in her work.
Guide her in her efforts.
Give her patience to dwell in spiritual practice.
Protect her from the darkness she is called to enter.
Clothe her in humor and humility.
Receive her into your life of love and peace.
Lord in your mercy,
Hear our prayer.

God, we trust in you above all. Protect us from danger and
draw us into your presence.
In Jesus' name, amen.

Katie Rasmussen ~ Who You Are and What They Don't Know ~

Who you are is powerful.
Who you are is needed.
Who you are is divine.
They don't know these things.
We see who you are.
We see what you offer.
We'll hold your hand.
We'll touch the pain softly.
You're safe with us.

Katy Drake Bettner ~

someday
in another life
the fear that ruled them will wane
the lamenting and gnashing will begin
as the true gravity of this failure becomes apparent
fear won
they will have to try again and again
you though
you will hear the refrain
well done thou good and faithful servant
your mother is proud
faith won

Kim Sandberg Turner ~

I wish that I could talk more of
spiritual complications
feminist injustices or just work up
a good scream into the cold night air.

I would join all my sisters in saying words
that would carry you
surround you
and maybe even lift you up.

But I am just stuck here
with my hands sitting on
a keyboard waiting for my fingers
to be told which letters to push.

Inside I feel a deepening sorrow
being paired with yours some
few thousand miles away,
because we both wanted to
walk and walk and walk and walk.

we believed the stories about
the boards with holes in them
and watched chewed gum
rubbed between two fingers.

We knew about store houses, vacuuming
long halls on Saturday afternoons
and how to decorate
a basketball court for a wedding.

We fed those in mourning
and visited women not like us.
We stood in holy places,

cooked in small kitchens and taught
in undecorated classrooms.

Our leadership was stored in little tiny closets
in narrow rooms with rows of cupboards
where behind each door was our calling
And inside each space, our tools.

We said yes, then soaked
our pillows with our tears…
and if and when we murmured,
we did it all in "two and a half" minutes.

We will miss nothing, and everything.
Bear witness, and cry foul.
Broken hearted, but not broken.
For we both know, don't we?

Kimberly Fitzpatrick Lewis ~

A blessing on your head through the Trees of the Loam of the Earth, the Stone of the Fire at its core, the Waters of every Shore:

When Mother speaks in tongues of wrath, she comes for the baby men who light the pyre of the acolyte. Your spirit dances away under the rain of Her love while they sputter and do not comprehend the Restoration is underway without them. Bless them, they know not what they do.

Kristen Shill ~ Worthy ~

He asked if I was worthy
with his thorny words.
I felt worthy of nothing, even life--

He asked if I was worthy.
I piled my whispered "Yes"
on the mountain of my fraud,
certain I spoke damnation to my bones.

"Worthy."
I will never be worthy.
Not that kind of worthy.

I create her in my image.
I ask the Goddess if I am worthy.
With tears in her eyes,
she wipes the word from my chin like vomit.

"My child, you are not worthy.
You are exquisite."

Laura Dickey ~ The Court of Sylvia ~

i.
Come in and sit down.
We love you very much;
love you enough to
upbraid you liberally,
fundamentally,
forever.

We speak for the Lord God
and after much prayer
(and a perusal of your social media)
have found that you are,
fundamentally,
problematic.

ii.
She left the office
And went to the woods.
She called out for God—
the one who wasn't,
fundamentally,
off Her rails.

iii.
Come daughter, let's dance--
I am so proud of you.
You are truth and bravery
and down to your marrow,
fundamentally,
magnificent.

Laura Lawrence ~

A blessing for Gina, my Mormon sister,
whose voice I know, because when she spoke
her words echoed across the ocean and fell in my lap.
And the words were brave and fierce and beautiful and told the truth.

I did not know before that we, my Mormon sisters and I,
could tell the truth and tell it loud.

But the brave ones knew, the poets and the prophesiers, and
they taught my lips to speak the truth,
quietly first (but to whom should I tell the truth more than to myself?),
less quiet now,
maybe one day fierce and beautiful and loud enough to
echo over mountains and through valleys and fall into laps.

And now I say, blessed are you, my brave sisters,
Blessed are you whose voices echoed, taught quiet lips to speak.

Laurie Anne Shipp ~ For Gina ~

How does one hold space for a dear one half a world away who is facing
banishment from the tribe that once was?
A dear sister whose spoken word and written prose so eloquently
described the thoughts and feelings so many of us share? "Yes, yes me
too" each time I listened or read.
Thoughts that reached out in earnest for a place at the table, efforts to
uncover the injustice, and a reaching out to that which holds the Divine in
our hearts.
Amid feelings of frustration, anguish, and an ever-present sense of
betrayal, she reminds us of that which is Divinely ours, that which is
Holy, and that which CANNOT be taken from us, for there is no need for
masculine intermediaries, we can walk our own roads, determine our own
Divine destiny towards that which is Holy.
She teaches of resolve, to reach for goodness, and to trust our own
determined soul.
She lights the dark corners of the treacherous path and assures that the
effort is worth it, that peace can be found.
She knows my own difficult story and I know hers. We share, we laugh,
we cry.
Tonight I hold space for my favorite Kiwi. I bless and honor her
consecrated journey.

Laurie Burk ~

Dearest Gina,

My heart is with you, but my words are caught somewhere between
continents; my mind is in a fog of jetlag and my thoughts are not
coalescing into what I wish I could say.

I hope someday we can stand together in the Hollow Square and feel the
voices lift us up. In the meantime, I will just share this, the blessing I
cannot articulate.

You have been a fierce and holy inspiration. You have been the prophet
on the wall. You are doing God's work; never let them tell you otherwise.
May God's grace attend you and may you always know His almighty
love will never grow weary of you.

With love,

Laurie Burk

Lesley Butterfield Harrop ~ Room Made For One More ~

Believers and doubters
in a room over-burdened
standing shoulder to shoulder
to witness
the Giver of miracles.
Friends carried one more
to the house
overflowing with
no room to enter in.
The door occluded
inclusion precluded
not room was made for one.
Friends carried
just one to the rooftop
above and from the heavens
they lowered a soul.
The healer said
Arise, take up thy bed,
and go thy way.
They found a way.
They made a way.
His love, this love; Is
room made for one more.

An infant's entrance
imminently arriving
with no room yet to prepare.
But room was made
in the most unlikely of spaces
because this would be His way.
They found a way.
They made a way.
His love. This love; Is
Room made for one more.

Refusals to bend for
fear of Losing their place
but place was made after all.

The Ceiling of sticks
shattered like glass and
the structure unyielding that
yielded to Him after all.
A blanket of hay
became his cradle
and throne.
A way provided
life and love divided.
When all seemed impossible
it was possible.
Room was made after all.

Lindsay Denton ~ The Hardest Part ~

The hardest part of patriarchy is not
that I am told what I cannot do;
it is that I am told
I cannot want
what I cannot do.

I am not allowed to want change
until after things have been changed:
retroactive wishing.

When even quiet desire
is an act of rebellion,
those who give words to the wanting
are brave as Esther
and wise as Eve.

Lindsay Hansen Park ~ For My Sister, Gina ~

We were taught to remember our ancestors. And we listened. Both of us, we listened and strained our ears to try to hear their calling to us from behind. To draw our strength from them, like the spoke of a wagon wheel- the draw of an oar, dipping into the water and salt, to cut through the earth on our way to where we belong.

Your people were the sea and mine were always trying to cross the ocean, never content to let the waves lap up on the shores and find home within ourselves. Somewhere along the border of land drifting down into sea, our people met and we called ourselves together, albeit peculiar. You and I-- we share a birthright, promises from those who came before. They promised us blessings and heaven if we could only heed their call.

And we did listen. It's not that we didn't try. It's just that within their voices we heard other voices too, and we learned to hear our own. Which is why I need you to know this too:

You are nobody's martyr. This is your birthright. This, your heritage, to pick up the oar and break direction where you are called. You are just doing what our people did, charting a course that calls to you.

You cannot be punished for it, though they will try. They always try, in their sad, brittle ways. They will get their plastic pens with their sticky black ink. Their folders and their binders and wooden desks and doors and offices. They will call that Power and pretend to wield it. They want you to play along and pretend it is power, too. A delete button in a database they call the Kingdom of God.

But we know differently. We have learned to be suspicious of those who try so hard to perform it. We have learned to pity and sometimes roll our eyes, because we see what they can't see: It's the things we are the most afraid of losing that we never had.

With every dip of your oar into the giant lake that is your life, that is Spirit, that is love--they demand you back--to tell you to stay the course, as if you could map a line into God. Because maybe if you can pretend that their power matters, then they can feel that their own rigid course is right, that their useless performance of sameness is best. They want us all to agree to the story they need to be right.

And I have tried sister, I have tried to make that story right. And I know you have as well. But we can't tell truths that were cut from the shame of so many men. Mormon women cannot be the receptacles of their shame, though they ask us to be.

Stay your own course. Use the strength and spirit from our ancestors--the ones where new experiences brought growth, not obedience. The ones where storms brought about strength, not loyalty. The ones where truth is only carved out from the muscle memory of experience. Stay your course and we will bear witness to you and to it.

All my love and power tonight. xox. You are mine and my people and always will be and always are.

Lisa Patterson Butterworth ~

It's pointless. They tell us.
You will never change them. They say.
We will not change. They declare.

****
They don't understand. Changing them never was the point.
*
We change ourselves.
*
Changing them, that is their journey.
*
We change ourselves.
*
We learned our voices don't matter.
Men speak with authority, women listen and obey.
And we were silent.
No.
*
We learn to speak for ourselves.
*
We learned righteous was not kindness, faith, or love, but knowing our
role.
They taught us our lives have meaning, purpose, direction.
They tell us
what meaning,
what purpose,
what direction.
We learned there is only one direction.
No.
*
We learn to direct ourselves.
*
We put on the role, the tiny role men tell us God made for us,
like a child's coat, much too tight, no room to move, no room to grow,
and it only comes in pink.
We sacrificed. We tried. We shrunk. We felt righteous. We said yes.
And if our hearts screamed no, we hid the secret shame that our role did
not fit,

hid that we were bad,
unworthy of love.
We cried in our closet and no one heard us or cared.
No.
*

We learn to trust ourselves.
*

They told us how good we looked in our tiny role, supporting them,
obeying them,
and it felt like acceptance, like love,
and we took Prozac and we smiled and insisted quite loudly,
"I love my role, I feel equal."
We believed it, because it was righteous.
We were invisible, even to ourselves.
No.
*

We learn to see ourselves.
*

When we could no longer shrink enough to fit our role,
when the heartbreak got too heavy to hide and when the empty sadness
leaked out the corners,
they said — women are incredible! Patted us on the head.
They tried to comfort us, to fix us.
No. They cannot.
*

We learn to fix ourselves.
*

We spoke, we cried out loud, brought our secret sorrow into the sunlight.
They called us our worst fear —
Unworthy. Unrighteous. Shameful. Broken. Power-hungry. Faithless.
Fake it. Be quiet. Hide yourself. Deceived.
You can't trust yourself.
Just leave.
A part of us still believed it, we've been trained to believe it.
No.
*

We learn to believe in ourselves.
***

It's pointless. They tell us.
You will never change them. They say.

We will not change. They declare.
Changing them was never the point.
They must learn to change themselves.
***

We learn to trust our faith,
Accept our divine nature,
Believe the promptings of our Heavenly Parents.
We teach each other.
Sisters in Zion.
*****

WE CHANGE OURSELVES.
(2014)

Lismarie Ellis Nyland ~

The worth of a woman?
Measured by a man?
He measures in assets and liabilities.
Measured by the goddess,
The worth of a woman is boundless and unbridled.

Maggie Hurst ~ Sisters ~

For Gina
Beloved.
Betrayed by fools.
They are mistaken, misled, confused, astray.
Your light is unlike
anything they have seen.
Your light warms the heart of the weary and
strengthens the afraid,
bringing hope to the lost and
igniting faith to be curious again.
It is the light of Mother God.
Through you, we see Her.
Shine on, beloved.
We are with you.

Malena Crockett ~ Calling Home ~

It's branding season again.
Molten tears searing, surging,
up,
out,
struggling to fill the gaping wound in my soul,
topple from their flooded precipice,
plummeting to perdition
before they can find their mark.
My sonic screams reach heaven.

Mother
– ever tuned to hear distress above the din –
Tenderly, so tenderly,
cloaks my broken heart
With a lullaby:

"Let them have their rules,
Their codes,
Their labels,
Their shame.
Know this -
You need not fit, nor bend
To heartless will.
Rise, breathe, live.
Shine. Glow.
Radiate.
Show them
You never were and are not theirs.
You are mine."

(Previously published on the *Exponent II* blog 15 October 2018,
https://www.the-exponent.com/guest-post-calling-home/.)

Mandy Lyons ~

Who says, of I, I am not yours--no mercy for the "me"s?
Who separates? Who segregates? Who builds blind and lifeless walls?
Vast gates burn, stone walls break
Who? They? THEY who?
Who is this "great" god They?

Oh! But I, I will honor HER. Will SHE hear me? Will SHE hear?
O, communion! Ah, my goddess! Merciful ray of the heart!
YOU shining shaft of brilliance
YOU eye of wisdom
YOU alliance, guardian of the law –

Who can perceive YOUR ways?

Peace? Who says "peace, peace" when there is no just peace?
The house of charm mocks my alarm. The tower of power devours and
rends.
Rivers run red, red, red with the blood of arrogance.
And for their thirst, their gall
For their hunger, rot of death

O! But I, I will honor HER. Will SHE see me? Will SHE see
The enslaved "I"s, the captive "me"s?
Who will restore; who will free?
See! all the fallen, SHE, yes,
SHE will gather each I, I, I, and me.

Who can perceive HER ways?

Who will ask you? Who will seek you? Who will eat from your tree?
Oh! But I, I will honor HER. Will she speak to me? Will she speak?
Come near me as I come near you
Swallow not intimate words
Uncover holiness and reveal

And reveal who can perceive your ways.

O, GREAT WEAVER
You gather me
You grasp these hands
You lift me
Clutch me to your breast
You know all of me
Who else can gather
Into the great river of life?
Nor arm of flesh
But by the spirit
Same dust, same dirt
There is no "other"
Let peace be as a river flowing to the sea
Oh! And I

MOTHER of me
You gather all the "me"s
You grasp meaning
You raise my spirit
Commune with my soul
       All of all the "me"s
All the drops of heaven
Not by might
Nor by power
But by breath of life
Same mud, same blood
       Who is not beloved
Let peace be as the current of eternity
I and all the "me"s

Untiring, Unceasing, Persisting, Everlasting, Unapologetic, Wild and
Free
If summer sun scorches, come the shade of your night
If winter wind blows, come the dawn of your day
Who can perceive your ways?

Margaret Olsen Hemming ~

To the God Who Sees Every Single One of Us:

May our sister know that she is not alone.
Help her to know that the seeds she has planted will bloom someday.
Help her to have wisdom as she navigates a new, unexpected path.
Help her to have hope that the times in which we wound one another will
pass away and be replaced with God's love.
Give her courage and peace when people tell her that she doesn't belong
in your family.
Most of all, grant her your grace. That is enough.

Marie Murphy ~ A Blessing, Sister ~

What does it mean
To speak a blessing over you?
Is it the words
That catch in our throat as we sit,
Stifled in the pews?
Do we pour out upon each other
All of the good gifts
That we wish heaven would send directly?
For you, dear sister
A blessing
A blessing for every good gift
And righteous endeavor
A noble spirit
And an upright zeal
A blessing of fervor
For you, sister
And then,
Once you have all of these things
That have been spoken over you
I bless that you
With the same fervor and zeal
Will burn it down
Every jot & tittle
And build
What *you'd* like to build
Instead

Marilyn Bushman Carlton ~ On Keeping Things Small ~

though I know
planting a terrarium
has something to do
with suppression I allow
myself to wallow
to delight in the sun
of my power to create
build permit life

fear necessitates
deliberate placement
of each similar
shade-tolerant two-inch
sprig of green
(one red for variety)
In this carefully planned
environment: a pyramid
of gravel charcoal treated
soil a little water

it takes work
to make plants think they thrive,
to make them lace and perk
a consistent sprinkling
to hide telltale wilting

overachievers must be pruned
anxious leafing
reduced to color-spots
small enough to position
reposition if necessary

this is no place for lush plants
whose large leaves cast shadows

even now brazen greens
press against containment

Maxine Hanks ~ The Marmalade Feminist Ward ~

Here, amid reconstruction attempts on
old houses and old minds, a thriving deconstruction
survives, deriving vitality from fallacies and facades
older than the city, misconstruction more ancient
than the neighborhood, more dangerous than shame
beneath faulty frameworks of tall buildings.

This resistance first existed in the silence
of troubled minds, found assistance in the nexus
of reality, crossed the lines of dogmatized duality
to holy space, eroding stones, undermining the
foundations of aging patriarchy.

Now, illuminating intuition's unformed passageways,
it lives, free and flourishing in the play between
what men and women say, inter-coursing
its way above conformity.

Priestesses stroll the streets, bless the residents,
serve a sacrament of wine, bread and poetry, fill the
empty halls with universal worship sung in silent songs,
hymns of human dignity.

Prophetesses see beyond the finite, past the future,
utter holy scripture, words of plenty for a congregation
of women, men and children, homeless
fallout of a nuclear family.

Here, fraternity and sorority mend archaic dichotomy,
find original complicity, in a peculiar community without
the Authority, conceived and born out of necessity
with a conscience immersed in forgiveness
for the suffering of its members,

and a clergy self-ordained
from a forsaken Mormon laity.

1990

(Published in the Mormon Women's Forum Quarterly, written while working on Women
& Authority, as a women's studies TA at the U of U, and living in the Marmalade Hill
neighborhood of Salt Lake City.)

Melody Newey Johnson ~ Prayer for the Planting of New Trees ~

Divine Mother, who holds us warm in
earthy womb, who bears the will of heaven
in both your hearts, hear our prayer.

Winter comes too soon this year,
the ground frozen, branches broken
with heavy wonder. (You heard the cry—

gravity multiplied while we slept,
felling hope harder than redwood.) You
know this ground. Your footprint is here

where now we tread. And not lightly.
Break the soil, Mother, drive blade thru
clay, make way for blood and root,

bud and stem, where newness snakes its
perfect path toward light. Your vessels:
veins of perfect rage and gentle future

leaf the world with green and golden love.
Breathe us in. Breathe us out. Grow us true
with every groan, ever reaching up, to life.

Melonie Cannon ~ Elements ~

Blessing from Earth:
>Bless the feet that walked through rich coals
>and burned fossilized footprints
> into the damp, dark earth.

Blessing from Water:
>Bless the hands that dipped in the bowl of light,
>cupped truth until it ran through spread fingers,
>dripped teaching into men's blind eyes.

Blessing from Fire:
>Bless the arms raised in protest-
>high flames like swords wounding the sky,
>burning the entrance door down.

Blessing from Air:
>Bless the mouth that spoke the healing prayer,
>smoke in undulating waves as wind over tall grass.
>Eyes couldn't see, ears didn't hear, lungs unfilled
>as the Breath of Life rolled over them.

Melonie Cannon ~ Mother Sings ~

When the stars are all counted
and the earth
does her final dance,
like a majestic chord,
your spirit will rise from its surface
and meet the hands of God.
She will say,

Daughter,
See the seeds you scattered
like glass shards into men's hearts?
now they are mighty obelisks
cut from the seer stone
of your life.
Holy witnesses of truth.
Come and see
what was woven in the spaces between the words--
black lines passing back and forth
on the page like a loom's shuttle.
This is where the power is--
in the gulps of air you inhaled
after each strike of the rod.
This is where you drank ME.

She will lay hands on your heart, daughter,
throw Her silver head back,
and sing your song
in higher courts.

Mette Harrison ~ From God and Goddess Both ~

Blessings on your questions,
Blessings on your doubt and uncertainty,
Blessings on your courage,
And blessings on your vision of truth.

She calls on me to tell you
That you are surrounded by her love.
Her arms are holding you up,
Though she trusts in your strength.

She calls on me to remember,
That you spoke of her to me first,
That you taught me courage,
And showed me the way of truth.

You walked ahead of me,
Allowing me to step in your big marks,
I have to hop because you took such distance in.
You saw the God ahead of you, beckoning.

Blessings on all of us who walk with you,
Who follow behind us, who walked ahead.
Blessings on those left behind,
Who say goodbye and good riddance.

Blessings from God and Goddess both.

Mindy Gledhill ~ Icarus ~
For Gina Colvin

What are those wings? What is that rust?
What are those tattered things that make you look like Icarus?
Somebody stole your fairy dust
And now the weight inside your chest betrays your wanderlust

So you fall into the waves
Of a thousand questions asked but none explained
And now all, all you can do
Is to trust that I'll be waiting here to carry you
I will carry you

Spectators come from far away
Like they have tickets to the circus on a Saturday
Caught like a child in a parade
You spread your arms but when you're wounded
You can't fly away

So you fall into the waves
Of a thousand questions asked but none explained
And now all, all you can do
Is to trust that I'll be waiting here to carry you
I will carry you

Smoke and feathers floating through the sky
Like the tears that you cry
Drops of melting wax rain down like fire
And you're so very tired

So you fall into the waves
Of a thousand questions asked but none explained
And now all, all you can do
Is to trust that I'll be waiting here to carry you
I will carry you

Mindy May Farmer ~ Echoes ~

For Gina.

Some voices cannot be silenced. The more you try to quiet them, the louder they echo; their power reverberating across oceans, mountains, deserts, and plains.

Women, especially, know how to amplify words patriarchy seeks to silence. We are disregarded as gossips; overreacting, overreaching, easily dismissed.

Women, relegated as diminutive versions of men, begin to minister by whispers, poetic prose, and a listening ear. Our voices tentative until She finds us and whispers:

You don't have to be broken to be better. You don't need to let go of you to become something more. You were never meant to be small.

We no longer whisper. Our voices become bolder. Braver. Fuller. She is with us and we are with Her. We minister in power and strength, unmoved by judgment or fear.

They see the power in our voices too late to mute us. Women, already on the fringes, pushed farther to the outside, labeled as other.

But some voices cannot be erased. Their power remains with the women who echo them; taking inspiration and hope; endowed in their own power. And new voices raise to join them.

Moana Uluave Hafoka ~ **For Gina** ~

I hold space with you, today
Like you held space with me

In a chance encounter
Two summers ago
From Fiji to LAX

At baggage claim,
Terror riding up my spine,
You stayed with me
In quiet communion

Waiting
As one man chose the fate of my husband and child

A choice of law and grace
A choice of stamping a piece of paper or severing family ties

I hold space with you, today
As you held space with me

Because discipleship
Is found in small
And hallowed spaces
Between women

'Ofa lahi atu,

Moana

Morgen Willis ~ A Midlife Anointing ~

Sister, hearing the call from God to minister to you by virtue of love, faith, sacrifice, and covenant, I place my hands upon you to anoint you in your pain.

I bless your head that you hair will not fall out from sorrow

I bless your mind, that it will function properly and not betray you

I bless your eyes that they will see true and clearly the light and darkness before them

I bless your ears that they may hear the music of your soul

I bless your bones that they will hold up your body and feel its rhythms

I bless your feet that they will take you through all the paths that you must walk

I bless your heart that it will beat

I bless your face that light will shine from your countenance, and that you will know what it is to be beautiful

I bless your teeth that they will be strong against the grinding

I bless your mouth that it will be a good servant to you

I bless your hands, that they will be productive and quick, that you may work hard and fast without tiring

I bless your soul with a will to live

I bless your ears that they will hear wisdom

I bless your blood, that it will course properly through your veins and fill you with life

I bless you with hunger for knowledge

I bless you with bravery, and courage in the face of all you learn

90

I bless you with faith and trust, and also vigilance and guile

I bless you with the wisdom of women, that you may navigate danger and Patriarchy

I bless you with friends, who will carry their burdens beside you, and love you when you are weak

I bless you with the gift of homemaking, that you may always have a place to go

I bless you with sunshine and rain, with valleys and peaks

I bless you with curiosity, that you may find joy and interest upon your journey

I bless your life with children, that you may rejoice

I bless you with sleep, that you may rest from each day

I bless you also with sleepless nights, that you may know solitude

I bless you with delight, with fragrant moments, with summer nights

I bless you, I bless you, I bless you.

In your pain, in your joy, I bless you.

You are blessed.

Nancy Ross ~ I Bless You with the Memory of Blessings ~

The children had gone to bed
The fire in the hearth was holding back
The chill mountain air
The women blessed each other
The specific words
Did not stick in my memory
But the things I felt during those hours
Never left.
A rare episode
Love from God and community
Revealed themselves together
In our bodies and words
A deep and abiding loving-belonging
Vibrant
Intense
Overwhelming
Sisters in need of comfort
The group serving as witnesses
Hands on heads shoulders knees feet
Hearing witnessing the sacred words.
I saw you blessing
Wielding this loving-belonging
Bringing your gentlest and strongest self
To this gift of compassion.

I cannot give you more
Bless you with more
Than what you showed us that night.
I can only say
Stay connected to that loving-belonging
I will do the same
Continue to share that gift
Be strengthened by it
Know that it is far too powerful
Your connection to it solid and sure
For some fool bishop to sever.

Natasha Helfer Parker ~ Punished ~

I am taught…
taught to stand…
on my own two feet.
Taught to choose,
with this agency they say I have.
Build up your OWN foundation!
Foundations of others won't work.
You can't borrow them I'm told.
Connection with the One above is the answer.
Willingness to the point of consequence is key.

Okay.
I believe.
So I stretch my feet…
I stretch my soul…
I take their words at face value…
I listen…
I study…
I practice…
I empathize…
I become knowing of this Christ creature.
I emulate Him…
In my own image,
I see.

But now I'm held suspect? Not welcome? Interrogated? Disciplined?
Why?
I'm deceived... they say. Under the influence.
I don't understand.
And then I do.

It wasn't about my relationship with God after all.
It was about their god.
In their image.
On their terms.
Not an agent after all… a conformer is what was wanted.

93

So I gather my strength…
my dignity…
and clothe myself with those as garments… as I shed the rest,
deciding or trying not to fear...
accepting of my raucous and willing laughter…
which pleasure was perpetually shamed.
I accept.
I love.
I live.

I tattoo it on my flesh,
even though I am forbidden.
I sear it as a brand,
lest I forget…
my virtue… my value… my worth.
"She is clothed in strength and dignity…
and she laughs without fear" is the scripture painted on my foot.
So I can stand in holy spaces… the spaces I occupy.

I will not fear.
He's my Christ now. Not theirs.
He's in my blood… flowing in my spirit...
mixed with His, and Hers, and His.
My Mormon deity is in my fiber... in my being.
The goal all along, I thought.
And yet,
now
I stand apart…
while all along inextricably connected.

Rewarded.

Nicole Thomas Durrant ~

I bowed my head and said Yes.
I will hearken unto my husband.
Surely, that can't be right?

When I finally reached the Celestial Room
to the excited faces of my family,
I pulled off my veil,
And turned away.

Week after week I went.
I read the books.
I prayed.
I asked the questions.

I never really noticed that before.
It will all work out in the end.
But he has to hearken unto God.
That's not a problem for me.

And yet, my husband did not ask or want me
To hearken unto him.
Is this how God saw me?

Year after year my soul crumbled
Under the covenant of hearkening.

On the early morning
Of my 40th birthday,
I left my sleeping husband and babes
And walked to the temple.

The darkness and lights of Los Angeles
Spread out before me.
I sat in front of the reflecting pool.
With the temple glowing behind me.

20 years had passed since I had
first taken the covenant.
At this very temple.

And I prayed.

With the crushing anguish that temple
had brought upon me.

I had so wanted it to be true.
I will never hearken unto a man.
The temple is no longer a holy place for me.

But I promised that I would always:

Be true and faithful to my husband.
To seek truth.
To love my children fiercely
To be honest and to
Love others.

And I was still.

And I waited.

God's love began to pour
From the heavens
Into my soul
And my spirit was on fire.
Light burst into my heart.
and my
mind was clear.
I began to cry.

I bowed my head and said Yes.

May you bow your head
My beloved sister
And say Yes

To God's love
May He pour into you
His light and goodness
And may you never hearken unto a man.

Olea Plum ~ And God was in the Thread ~

I choose the thread carefully,
      it will stitch the fabric together,
            the fabric I cut apart
            because (I know) it will look better
            when it's rearranged,
      the bright floral
      neighbouring bold stripes

            I cut the fabric apart
and lay contradictions together,
for each to seem more clearly
what it is

I choose the thread carefully
      for the top and the bottom
            (sometimes they shouldn't be the same)
      to join the layers together and make a quilt

            I cut the fabric apart
because too much of the same is boring

I choose the thread carefully
      to hold everything together
            (together and apart
            each piece its own self
            every piece required
      to make a beautiful whole)

Olivia Meikle ~

My heart is breaking, and joyful, and sorrowful, and so full of hope.
Because this is not the same world it was.
And though they do not understand this,
they cannot silence your voice.
They cannot silence our voices.
Our God, that these men of power will never understand, will never be
severed from you. From any of us.

You remain, the stubbornly beating heart of our little corner of the Body
of Christ.

**Page Turner ~ A Tableau from Power and Restraint: A
Feminist Perspective of Mormon Sisterhood ~**

Rachel Farmer ~ Untitled, Pencil on Paper, 2008 ~

Rachel Hunt Steenblik ~ Lament ~

Gina knows the Mother,
knows the women
standing outside gates
crying, lamenting across
large walls.
She says, *Name it.*
Name it. Again and
again and again.
Name the Mother.
Name the lament.
Name the wall.
Say it until they
can't ignore it.
Until they listen.

Raini Hamilton ~ A Mormon Blessing ~

Sister,

By the power I hold as a believer in Holy Divinity and as a fellow traveler in this collective dream, I bless you.

I bless you with clarity of mind, that you may see your past, present, and even future clearly. That this sight will give you strength and dignity as you walk the path before you.

I bless you with abundant courage -- the courage to allow yourself to cry and truly mourn, the courage and strength to weather your grief.

Sister, I bless you with great strength as you rise from your place of mourning.

I bless you with power as you continue to be honest and vulnerable in your journey. You are a light bearer to others who walk similar paths. You sacrifice much to offer this light to others. Our Mother sees you. She is moved by your offerings and willingness to walk with Her.

I bless you with a steady heart. I bless you with peace that will radiate from inside you. This peace will be a balm of healing for yourself and your family.

You are a beautiful soul and eternally loved. This knowledge burns bright within you. No man will dim your inner sun.

I offer you these blessings and any others our Mother-God sees fit. In Her blessed name, amen.

Rebecca de Schweinitz ~ Sisters in Zion: A Reflection ~

Mary
Insisted on treating women
Like rational creatures, instead of flattering their fascinating graces, and viewing them as if they were in a state of perpetual childhood.

Elizabeth
Identified
A long train of abuses and usurpations
Imposed on woman by man, in contrast to
The enlarged sphere which her great Creator has assigned her.

Harriet
Decried the
Habits of submission that make men as well as women servile-minded and *customs that harden human beings to any kind of degradation, by deadening the part of their nature which would resist it.*

Emma
Called every woman to reject *external* and *internal tyrants*
To stand firmly on her own ground and to insist upon her own unrestricted freedom, to listen to the voice of her nature.

Yosano
Warned
All the sleeping women
Are now awake and moving.

Virginia
Taught women to
Look upon society, so kind to [men], so harsh to us, as an ill-fitting form that distorts the truth; deforms the mind; fetters the will.

Simone
Asked the essential questions
How can a human being in woman's situation attain fulfillment?
How can independence be recovered in a state of dependency?
What circumstances limit women's liberty and how can they be overcome?

How did this all begin?
How is it that the world has always belonged to the men?

Pauli
Called for a new
Self-definition
Nurtured from within rather than imposed from without. And for
*The redistribution of power and wealth—among black and white, rich
and poor, men and women, old and young, red and brown and all the in-
betweens.*

Betty
Told women to
Believe the voice inside herself, [even and especially] *when it denies the
conventional, accepted truth by which she has been living.* To
Create, out of her own needs and abilities, a new life plan.

Monique
Imagined a *Revolution*, a
*Conceptual reevaluation of the social world, its whole reorganization
with new concepts, from the point of view of oppression.*

Adrienne
Named
The specific subjection of women, through our location, in a female body.

Gloria
Uprooted, *transcended*, duality with
*Divergent thinking characterized by movement away from set patterns
and goals and toward a more whole perspective, one that includes rather
than excludes.*

Laurel
Reclaimed <u>The Church</u>
It is *not an ascending hierarchy of the holy. It is millions of ordinary
people calling one another "brother" and "sister" and trying to make it
true.*

106

Sonja
Prayed, and heard
"Patriarchy is a sham"
And *began to understand that God is not going to punish women for
thinking, for questioning, for seeing through the myths that bind us, for
being angry about what so richly deserves our anger, for going forth
boldly to fight against the injustices that have been visited upon us so
casually and cruelly for so long.*

Gina
Joined her sisters
Building
Comforting
Strengthening
Fulfilling

Reija Rawle ~ A Priestess Blessing (to be kept folded up somewhere near to your heart) ~

i bless you to wake in the morning to the rhythm of the tide
warblers flying north along ancient wind-born routes
sunlight rushing in from centuries past
your own heart beating

i bless you to run fast in the rain until you can't run
anymore your lungs burst and you stop
just breathe in the drunkenness
i bless you to be soft
soft as your baby skin the day you were born
soft as your breasts whose milk has come, and gone

i bless you with courage
to make peace with your mother
to take up your needle and sew a quilt with small scraps

for what you seek is not a home but an orbit--
a kaleidoscope, not the stars
and the rocket you built
it's not for flying
but falling

and to love,
you must sing loudly
the lullaby-tune of the earth
her polyphony of seasons erupting
bringing old comforts and somehow, new lights

so i bless you with courage
to make peace with your daughter
to take up your needle and sew a quilt with small scraps

i bless you to walk slowly in the rain, mouth open
as the waters carve a deep well in your heart
be still as others come to drink
i bless you to find grace

i bless you to sleep in the evening to the rhythm of the tide
warblers flying south along ancient wind-born routes
starlight settling in from centuries past
your own heart beating

RevaBeth Russell ~ Microburst ~

There they stood.
A cluster of six tall evergreens
Stalwart, straight, stately.
One day they were gone
Exposing a raw hole to the sky.
I often go back
Still feeling their absence.
They called it a microburst.
I knew it was excommunication.

Sally Peel ~ For Gina Colvin ~

An apple-green truth
So bright! She can't unsee it
We have found our way

Sara Burlingame ~

I
Dear Gina,
Fuck them.
Love,
Sara

II
Hey Girl,
I heard, like, across the Atlantic, what they wanted to do to you.
It's so funny what they don't know. What they'd figure out if they ever
came to the trailer park or detention for bad kids: we'd probably listen if
you were kind to us for even a second.
I hope your teenage self is beating in your badass heart and reminding
you of the ferocity that got you through the first, second, and infinity
times.
You got this,
S

III
My Sister,
I won't brush my hair for a week. I'll tell my sons the story you told us
about the little Maori girl who brought back the moon. I wish I knew how
to not be hurt by these broken men, but I don't. How dare they, I whisper.
The Wyoming wind steals the whisper and carries it far away. How dare
they.
All my love,

Sara

Sara Hughes-Zabawa ~

May you be blessed to wipe away the misunderstanding of others as you step further into the clarity of what you know is true, what is just, and what is real.

May you be blessed to look down at your feet and smile as you remember the path your soul chose to walk, without asking you if you were fully ready. Trusting the earth underneath you, that this path was where you needed to go, for your heart to break wide open, and to bow down to the not knowing and to meet the All-Knowing.

May you be blessed to feel the love of others carry you across the battlefield of this broken institution. May our love carry you like wings and lay you gently on the shores of our gratitude. It is there we would laugh, and cry, and mourn with you, for we too know what it feels like to be shunned, to be misunderstood, to be cast out. And yet it is in our own un-belonging we found you, and that has been the greatest gift. Following your insight, it was the map to belonging to ourselves for the very first time.

May you be blessed to know you have healed broken souls on your journey. Know without question your ministry has been one of love coupled with the dangerous permission to seek a life of spiritual health and wellness. If one's invitation is to awaken to one's heart and to bravely begin to wonder again, that is a battle cry worth answering.

May you be blessed to know, in every fiber of your being, that one person wielding pretend power does not have the ability to erase what is already cosmically created.
Connections are not so easily severed.
They can no more snuff out the stars as they can untangle the love that binds you to your beloveds. When will they learn that love is a force that can't be so easily cut?

May you be blessed to know when to rest, when to lead, and when to lean on those who love you. May you be blessed to know this changes everything and nothing and that tomorrow you will be just as loved as today. May you be blessed to know you are never alone, your sisters are here, ever beside you.

May you trust you are exactly where you need to be.

113

Sara Katherine Staheli Hanks ~

Part of me wonders:
who am I to bless you?

You were born before me.
You walked ahead of me.
You walk paths I never will.
You answer questions
I haven't even learned to ask,
and you move like fire and water
somehow held together,
and you scare away shame
with the tiniest word.
I don't know what my words can do.

But I do know
that I sat curled
in my mother's womb one night,
and while I did,
she sat straight
in a pew
and listened to a man of God
tell her
(tell all the women there)
to go home.
Stay home.
Make home a heaven on earth.
Come away from worldly pursuits
and fulfill the measure of your creation.

I was born the next morning
in a snowstorm.

I know that I came into this world,
away from my heavenly home,
and I needed women to teach me.

Thank you for being one of them.

114

Thank you for making this earth your home
and giving your voice to all of us.

I bless you.

I bless you because
we inhabit a common earth
and share a common home --
a church we loved.
Loved.
Love,
in a way.
And that loved us back.
In a way.
For a while.

I bless you
in mistake, in triumph,
in stillness, in speed,
in pain, in solace.

I bless you
to fill the measure of your creation.
Only yours.

I bless you
to find home in every place
where love presides,
where courage speaks,
where laughter is welcome and plentiful.

Who am I to bless you?

I am your sister,
and you are mine,
and we share a home,
and I am blessed because of it.

Susan Howe ~ The Hag of Beara ~

Twice the size of an ordinary mortal,
she sits on her haunches, arms resting
on her knees, a shawl about her
made of whatever you see—cloud,
sheepskin, rough-spun wool, draped
seaweed. She watches the town,
the bony hills, Mishkish behind them,
the bay, waves frothing to escape.
Watches the moon rising, or the sun.
Salt-coated eyelashes sometimes
alter what she sees.

No wave breaking can move her,
no hurricane. Winds that blow gulls
onto the cliffs she scarcely feels.
But the suffering—so heavy.
Only granite could bear it,
she's become granite. To see
the wounded wander the world.
She already knows,
has seen them cross oceans,
mountains, bogs, hoping to rest
their foreheads against her.

I have the sight, she says. What happened to you,
happened to me. What's done cannot be
undone, you suffer and I suffer.
And though there is misery
in this world, and guilt, there is also grace.
Touch the crags of my face,
feel my love for you yourself. Earth love,
bedrock, permanent love.

The pilgrims sit for a while, then turn back,
find the road to Eyeries, then on through
Castletownbere. Some wash themselves
in the sea, slough off her touch. Most
carry her, though she won't leave her cliff,
with them into the future
along twisting, narrow roads.

Susan Krueger-Barber ~ Key ~

Dear Gina, you are key.

Mind palaces maze, deep souled within
room by room multitudinous locked invisible doors.
Your voice, pocketed energy plugged waves
arrowing up inside our ears.
Turn and unturn door knobs.
--P--U--L--L--
break instinct vast open to newfangled bright spaces.

Circuitous paths,
inquiry beyond destination, cul-de-sacs travel turning.
We want no finish.
Oh, the lackluster disappointment of *finish*.
Life blood is inquiry, searching, investigation!
New rooms.
Possibility! Possibility! Possibility!

Dear Gina, you are key.

Tamra Wright ~ W-HOLE SEPA-RATION ~

Take away from me

a piece that was once
the center of my beginnings
an identity that felt solid
felt sure.
But it is only a piece,
not the whole
of who I am.
It will not leave a hole
in the center of my frame,
it will be space for new
color and lines and stories
that are filled by a universe
of possibilities ....

Taylor Carver Kevan ~ The Whale's Instinct ~

We must have the whale's instinct,
As we swim in unruly seas that wish us extinct.
When they try to separate one from the pod,
Claiming to do so in the name of God,
The ninety and nine send out our vibrations
So that not one soul gets lost in translation.

Rise, like the whale above storm-tossed sea,
Alight in the sparkling air and call out! God amplifies
Our voices charting courses amid the debris
Buoying up each soul men seek to agonize.

As the waves ebb and flow us assort,
God, Herself will be our support.

She will preserve us
Upon the waters of the deep,
While they may defame us
Wishing us back into sleep…

Awake! Sleep means slowly drowning alone.
Courage! The God whose waves roar, who divided the sea
Witnesses in the deep our grief, heavy like a millstone.
Her life-giving embrace cuts the cord, sets us free.
The Heavenly Mother of Hosts hears our plea.

Sister, swim on.
Together,
We'll greet the dawn.

Tresa Edmunds ~

We have always been here.
Thrumming under the surface.
Doing the work that goes unobserved.
The painstaking piecing of hearts and quilts.
The tender administrations that bind wounds
And lives.
Words, with their patient, gentle beckoning
Leading spooked horses to Living Waters.
In this world the glory goes to the gory.
The woundmakers.
The bombthrowers.
The ones who find power in domination,
And tell themselves that makes them impervious.
But underneath, always,
there were women.
Women who sweat and screamed them into life.
Women who repaired their path of destruction.
Women who tended to the broken
whose bodies and souls were sacrificed to voracious need.
Women who will meet them as their bodies fail.
Women who will comfort them out of this world.
Women who bear record.
Women at the well and women as witnesses to resurrection.
They believe power is proven by what it can break.
They will never see the transcendence
That comes from power that restores.

Twila Newey ~

you still know
what you've always known
to watch a flower open at dawn
is to watch god breathing
every other thing is just humans
stitching their various stories
into flesh of senseless suffering.

Wendy Christian ~

You are my friend, my sister, my mentor.
"Auntie" to my daughters.
You empowered me to speak truth to power,
To stand in my own power,
To create a healing narrative for the
deepest pain in my heart.
My mother wound.

You inquired about my tears
in the mountains of Colorado.
This moment ended in uproarious laughter about our
strikingly similar life journeys.
And about men and marriage and
motherhood.
(The joy and the struggle of it all.)
About loving a church that does not return
that love to us.

You have championed me.
You have inspired me.
You have been there for me
in the best and worst of times.
You care deeply about the well-being
of my daughters.
This is a gift I have no words for.
It fills me.

You have planned and led women's retreats
on the Feminine Divine with me.
Reluctantly at times, but you took my vision
and made it a beautiful reality.
Those retreats changed me.
They changed the women who attended.
Your generosity made them possible.
The Mother was there.
I was healed.

We have shared pho in NYC and sung
the night away at a piano bar

122

in the West Village.
Spontaneously, we hit a Broadway show.
We shared big feelings at
the 9/11 Memorial Museum.
You opened my eyes even more.

And now I offer a blessing:

Mother Father, God and Goddess,
Please bless my friend,
Gina Marie Rahwiu Colvin.
Encircle her in your love.
Enfold her in your ever-loving arms.
Protect her from the harm
church men would wield at her.

Embrace her **Nathan** with all that you are.
Grant him your protection and endless love.
Give him the wisdom
to know how to navigate his journey.
Keep their blessed union safe and whole.

Give their boys the sun and the moon.
Guide them. Lead them.
Rescue them from their hurts.
Bless their parents with the attunement to
ascertain their needs.
Spread love across each heart in this
gorgeous family.

I bless you, Gina, with the strength
of your mountain.
With the power of the woman
who hung the moon.
With everything that I am
and that I hope to become.
With all the love in my heart.

Your friend, always,
Wendy xx

Epilogue ~

On the 7th of December I received my formal notification of the Church Discipline from my Bishop. This was after six months of warnings and laborious discussions. It arrived as Nathan and I were sitting down to dinner. I saw the PDF of the letter pop up on my phone screen with a note to say that the paper copy would be delivered in person the next day.

I cried.

"Nathan, can we just drive up to Bishop's now and give him my letter? I'm so, so tired of this. Don't make me go through this."

His eyes too filled with tears, and I was newly outraged that this was his burden as well.

"I'm done with this," I wept. Nathan took my hand and said with compassion and sincerity,

"OK. Let's go up there tonight. We'll give him the resignation letter and it will be all over."

"Are we going to be OK?" I asked him.

"Yes," he said. "I choose us."

There was a manner in which he said this which was a breath of freedom. I knew down deep that we'd be fine and that he had chosen us years ago, but I think few Mormon marriages are contracted with that caveat. The one that says,

"If you should have a faith crisis and pull away from the church enough to jeopardize your standing in it, there's enough juice and love and affection in this for our marriage to survive. I will commit to love you with or without the church."

Partners in Mormon marriages are bound by a mutual duty and obligation to stay in the church. That's the way they begin, and that's the way they are supposed to end. But, here we were, on that Friday evening with my letter of summons to a discipline with enough care and respect and love for each other that we were able to confidently choose each other with or without the church. That might sound asinine to observers of Mormonism, but it means a lot to us, because we know, deep down, that getting married 'in' the church really means getting married 'for' the church, 'with' the church, 'including' the church and 'loyal' to the church. Just having that realization gave me the wind of relief that I needed to say, 'It's OK. I won't resign. I just won't go to the council.'

When I publicly announced the date of my discipline, I was surprised by the outpouring of concern. I was contacted by many people asking what they could do. I batted each of their offers away.

'It's OK. I think I always knew this would happen.'
'No, I really don't want a vigil in Salt Lake City.'
'Please don't make an #IstandWithGina meme.'

On so many levels it felt very private. But I knew that because I had shared this journey with so many others over the years, it was personal for them as well, so I had to respond to their need to be involved, but I was unsure of how. I was talking to my friend, Natasha Helfer Parker, who implored me for something to do. On a whim I told her,

"If you would like to ask people to send letters of witness or support of me to my bishop and stake president, I would really appreciate that." I was not really imagining that this might become a reality, but Natasha set to work and the letter writing began. At the same time, Joanna Brooks reached out, and knowing me as she does, she wouldn't take 'no' for an answer. So, I told her that what I really wanted was for this to begin a book of blessing and poetry for women in the church who had been disciplined or hurt by the church. And suddenly the poetry and the blessings flooded in. "Mormon women are impressive," I thought again. "These are the best women I know."

Soon I was getting surprised messages and emails from friends all over the world who told me that both my bishop and stake president had responded very graciously to their letters of support for me. I was surprised as well, and secretly pleased that some New Zealand leaders were doing what American leaders seem incapable of doing: reaching out and showing kindness. Some were ecstatic!

"I heard from your bishop and stake president." They effused. "They seem really nice!"

"Don't be their friend," I replied churlishly.

A few days before the 20th December, the day that my discipline had been scheduled for, my friend Melissa in Auckland contacted me. "I'm coming to meet your bishop. I don't think it will do much good, but I'll try." "O…Kay..???" I thought.

And then she followed up with, "And I'm proposing that we meet together for dinner. Let's take the issue of discipline off the table and just take in turn to share how we came to our deepest faith." "I can't do that." I replied. "The thought of it makes me sad."

Melissa can be convincing, and so on the day before, I picked her up at the airport and dropped her off at Bishop Josh's office with a laptop in hand and a sixty slide PowerPoint presentation on what a miserably bad decision it is for the health of the church to discipline for apostasy. After an hour, they emerged chatty and friendly, and then Nathan, Melissa, Bishop Josh, and I headed out to dinner together in our car, all the while keeping up a witty banter about the next day's discipline. For the next hour we shared food and our testimonies. It was strangely lovely.

Instead of attending the discipline, I had planned an evening of 'intentional spiritual non-violence.' My priest Megan was going to come by and hold a Eucharist with myself and friends, and we were going to eat together and talk about what brings us hope, joy, peace and love. After all, it was Advent. We had agreed that we would not give the discipline any attention. Nathan was going to the discipline, and we'd just wait for him to come home with the result. Nathan had spent the evening preparing his arguments. My former bishop, Pete, was also attending on my behalf. His own children would be deeply affected by an action against me, so his reasons were both supportive and personal. But, the rest of us at home, with candles burning, and good food before us, would be under instruction not to speak a word of LDS Church until Nathan returned. I imagined us creating sacred space together, and just the

127

thought of friends and song, and love, felt both healing and wonderfully subversive.

But, at around midday, I received a message from my bishop. While I hadn't told him of my intentions for the evening, Religion Dispatches and the Salt Lake Tribune both ran the story. I'd also had an extended interview with John Dehlin on Mormon Stories Podcast, so it was well known that I wouldn't be attending.

His request was sincere. Would I please show up, not for a discipline as such, but to see if we could build a bridge of understanding rather than a wall of division? There was a manner in his request that suggested a shift and a softening. I sat with the question for the next couple of hours, mulling it over and praying on it. I had an online Advent study class at 3:00 p.m. and told them of my conundrum. In turn, my friends shared their thoughts and worries with me. And then we talked about the Journey of Love and the place of friends as we take that path.

I sat in contemplative prayer with this question. I laid the question out and then fell into stillness as I opened myself to Divine presence.

When I opened my eyes, I knew what I should do. But, I cried, "Why do I have to do hard things?" I don't know if there is a word for simultaneously feeling both outrage and loving relief at the direction I should take. But, that's how I felt. It felt a very difficult, right thing to do, and I had both irritation and consolation from that.

We arrived at the meetinghouse to a small group of friends who we had originally invited to our evening of spiritual non-violence. Having been uninvited when our plans changed, they decided that they wanted to show up at the church and be close by while Nathan, Pete, and I were in the next room.

So, they pulled up chairs into a circle in the Primary room while we went into the room opposite and closed the door.

I want to say something about the spiritual effect of having friends. During the council, I was sometimes aware of the steady murmur of my friends' conversation from the other room. I heard them laughing, sometimes one voice would be speaking alone, at times there were surges of excited chatter. And all of it was lovely, as if their friendship was leaking under the door, right into my heart. On top of this, I was mindful of the candles, the prayers, the poems and the blessings I had received, too many to number. All of it, I choose to believe, created what I can only describe as a crystal halo of love. It was so tangible and dense in that moment that at times I would lose my concentration because I was being held in a vapour of goodness that was thick and rich with deep hope and kindness.

I'm used to 'handling' things independently. I don't attach easily to people. I'm not needy. I never draw waters from dry wells of friendship. I alarm myself at the easiness by which I can walk away. But, this cloud of goodness, this force field of well-being and concern that was being directed on my behalf felt as real as anything I have ever felt in my life. If nothing else, that one collective energy of prayer and blessing that held me so tenderly healed a loneliness in me. For that alone, going to my disciplinary council would have been worth it.

My bishop set down a thick stack of papers beside him. After a prayer to open, he said,

"I've read each of these letters, and I've been very moved by them. I'm sorry. But, I don't think I really understood when I started this process. Now, I think I better understand."

Bishop went on to say, "Let's see if we can have a conversation with mutual respect. And if you feel that this council becomes dominated by my authority, then I would completely understand if you left."

And then we talked.

And pretty soon it was just Bishop and I, moving through our concerns and our vulnerabilities, carefully laying our cards out on the table. Tears flowed freely, explanations were offered, apologies were made, and when there was nothing left to say, Nathan and Pete and I left the room for the council to confer.

I was not surprised that the outcome was "no action." For it to have been anything else would have been a betrayal of something lovely and kind and profoundly Christlike that we had generated together. Pete, my former bishop, burst into tears. His daughter was in the other room ready with her letter of resignation if I had been excommunicated. We all hugged each other, knowing that what was done was good. It was very good. Church disciplines are terrible things and I wish they would be struck down, and I'm not saying that I support them in any way. But, what happened that night felt significant.

"No action."

I sat with the importance of that for a moment, and while everyone present was subdued with good and loving feeling because of how right a thing it was, I thought,

'Oh no. It looks like this church and I are still stuck with each other.'

Gina Colvin, February 2019

Gina Colvin ~ A Blessing on Those Who Would Excommunicate ~

When the nerves jangle, sparked alive with sweaty irritation,
At the nerve of it all,
And you explode with charged ferocity at every challenge to what is,
Snapping in fermenting defensiveness.

When rivulets of that apostate's resistance begin to shake your river of
religious fixity
And your resentment deepens
Trapping you into daggered imaginations of revenge,
Inflamed by your sureness.

When a challenge is raised to all that you had thought was unassailable,
And you arm yourself with the technologies of discipline,
Ready to launch the counter-attack from the ramparts,
With the polished heavy artillery from the church's magazine.

And when the order of things is made questionable,
By another's clever wit that brought alive an attentive audience,
Who now leave the fragrance of their displeasure,
Over the treasury of a church you thought it was your duty to guard.

When you,

March too readily to the drum beat of authority,
Excuse too quickly the tendency to double-talk,
Become too pre-occupied with the performance of the people,
Control too rigidly the outbreaks of dissent,
Demand too bullishly the marks of uniformity,
Think too highly of the exclusivity of your faith,
Command too threateningly the secrecy of the church's machinations,
And miss too overtly the point of the Gospel.

Put down your weapons,

And look with compassion at the One.
Then look at the one who has aroused the ferocity in you so murderous
you have failed to see their humanity.

131

He is the former bishop whose files are filled with proof that he'd been betrayed,
She is the humble historian with a story to tell gathered from the dusty archives of too soon forgotten evidences,
He is the meticulous professor who assembled the data and told important stories from it,
She is the concerned grandmother who just wanted justice for her grandbabies,
He is the outraged lawyer who saw your heavy handedness and had to speak up,
She is the young one who thought women had much more to offer than was allowed them,
He is the clever computer whizz who wondered if transparency would be the best disinfectant,
She is the writer, who assiduously kept records that pointed to a pattern of ecclesiastical abuse,
He is the older gentleman who simply wanted our children protected,
She is the young missionary who was left with the scars of abuse when the president put his hands on her,
He is the gay man who believes that around God's table all humanity deserves to stand, including his children.
She is the indigenous woman who wants the church to stop robbing her and her family of their identities.

Put down your weapons,

And see the one.
Then look again and see the One,

Who, against the perversions of Empire and the religious elite,
Stood completely alone,
On a cross,
Made by hands similar to yours.

So, my angry friend,
Put down your weapons of institution,
Unless you too want to be found guilty of stoning the prophets.

Author Biographies (in order of appearance) ~

Joanna Brooks is the author or editor of ten books, including *The Book of Mormon Girl* (2012), and *Decolonizing Mormonism*, which she co-edited with Gina Colvin (University of Utah Press, 2018). Mormon feminism is her spiritual home.

Alisa Bolander is a professional instructional designer and was formerly a regular blogger at *Exponent*. She believes in community and lives in Sandy, UT with her family.

Amanda Farr is an exceptional human being who currently resides in San Diego, California. When she is not working or pursuing a master's degree, Amanda is a phenomenal parent to and advocate for her four beautiful children. If she's not at home, Amanda will likely be found at Disneyland, sportsing, or in Pittsburg.

Amy Lynn Pierce Caston is the second of four daughters, wife of one husband, and mother of three children. She comes from a long line of strong women. Amy is a native and current resident of northern California. She earned a BA in Theatre Arts from Brigham Young University and a teaching credential from San Francisco State University. Amy is a middle school theatre teacher, a second-degree black belt in Taekwondo, and a lover of fantasy and science fiction. When she grows up, Amy plans to be the village crazy lady. She hopes to travel the world, and seeks greater spiritual enlightenment.

Amy Rich is a 48-year-old wife, mother, sister, daughter, aunt, niece, friend, neighbor, stranger, but most of all, she is a woman. The more she learns, the less she realizes she knows, but she owns her experiences because they have led her to new loves, new thoughts, and new adventures. She is learning to live in the present with compassion and no judgement. Living in the moment, laughing with her family and friends, and taking time to create, connect, and think critically, brings her joy and gives her purpose.

Annalicia Whittaker used to be a good Mormon girl; now she's just a girl who is Mormon (and many other things--thanks to the mentors, philosophy teachers, and therapists that taught her to ask, "who decides?"). She's studying psychology, teaches Primary 7s, loves to try new things, and hails from Oregon. She currently lives in Portland, in a crappy apartment, with her husband and an adopted feral-cat named "Tack".

Ariel Wootan Merkling is a thirty something mother of two who enjoys social work, libraries, and making tamales. Dislikes include whales, laundry, and writing bios. Her advice to new writers is be good, but not too good, or you might have to talk about yourself in a bio.

Ashley Mae Hoiland is the author of *100 Birds Taught Me to Fly*, and creator of several projects, including the We Brave Women cards. She currently lives with her husband and three small children in Santa Cruz, CA.

Blaire Ostler is a philosopher and leading voice at the intersection of queer, Mormon, and transhumanist thought. She is a board member and former CEO of the Mormon Transhumanist Association, the world's largest advocacy network for the ethical use of technology and religion to expand human abilities. She presents and writes on many forums, and speaks at conferences promoting authentic Mormonism. Blaire holds a degree in design from the International Academy of Design and Technology-Seattle. She is currently pursuing a second degree in philosophy with an emphasis in gender studies.

Brittany Romanello is a daughter, a survivor, a listener, a seeker, and a believer. She is a doctoral student in Anthropology at Arizona State University. Her current research focuses on highlighting the social and parenting experiences of undocumented Latina mothers in the Church. She holds out great hope for Mormon womxn worldwide, and says, "as we advocate for and bless each other, our tender experiences will be seen, validated, an embraced while we journey on in our faith, wherever it may take us."

Callie Ngaluafe is a hiker, swimmer, dancer, and lover of the natural world. She writes poetry and fiction, and she eats semi-sweet chocolate chips while reading novels in her bed at night.

Carol Lynn Pearson began her Mormon writing career with the publication of a slim book of poems titled *Beginnings*. She has since contributed numerous books, plays and lyrics, many of which address the challenging issues of accepting our LGBTQ sisters and brothers. An ongoing theme has been transforming patriarchy into partnership, evidenced in such works as *The Ghost of Eternal Polygamy* and her one-woman play, *Mother Wove the Morning*, in which she plays sixteen women throughout history in search of God the Mother.

Cheryl L. Bruno has a BS in recreation management from Greensboro College, Greensboro, N.C. She enjoys all water sports and coaching swimming. Cheryl is an independent researcher on Mormon history, with an interest in the intersection of Mormonism and Freemasonry. She has published several articles, poems, and personal essays. Her current project is a book titled *Method Infinite: Freemasonry and the Mormon Restoration,* to be published by Kofford Books.

Christa Baxter is a Utah expat whose Mormonism was shaped by growing up in the Bible Belt. Utah has been home since she moved to Provo in 2005 to attend Brigham Young University. Though she's still surprised to find herself in the Jell-O Belt all these years later, the mountains, family, and her friendships with local Mormon feminists have made it all worth it. When she's not writing poems or blog posts decrying the silliness of the patriarchy, she's playing guitar, hiking, reading, knitting, or spending time with friends and family.

CJ Obray, Seattle author, photographer, poet, and feminist, was raised in a traditional Mormon family in a "typical" Mormon-corridor community. For better and worse, she followed the path laid before her. Now she writes about the Mormon female experience, examining themes common to us all. Mormon women's voices and gifts are often overlooked and at risk of being silenced or lost forever. CJ writes to keep those voices alive. When she's not working on her own projects, CJ moderates BadDay Memes on Facebook, and she helps other writers as The Boss at *wipWizard.com*.

CJ Schneider is the mother of three and author of *Mothers of the Village: Why All Moms Need the Support of a Motherhood Community and How to Find It for Yourself.* CJ is at heart an explorer, keen to learn all she can about truth, love and life.

Cynthia Bailey Lee has written about intersections of feminism and Mormon life for *Exponent II* magazine and at *By Common Consent*, where she is a regular blogger. By day, she is a Lecturer on Computer Science at Stanford University, where she teaches technical courses in the theory and practice of computer science, researches engaging and culturally-responsive teaching practices, and advocates for diversity and social responsibility in the high-tech industry. She lives in Palo Alto, California, USA with her husband, two children, a cat, and chickens.

Danna Myers Hook is a daughter, sister, friend, wife, and mom. She has four awesome kids. She loves gardening, knitting, Shakespeare and Mary Oliver. For nine years, she has been an advocate and cheerleader for breastfeeding families, and she continues learning in order to help more families in her community. Mormonism is her cultural language and heritage as much as her Scandinavian, British Isles, and German heritage is. Originally from San Diego, she now calls Northern Nevada home.

Dayna Patterson is the author of *If Mother Braids a Waterfall*, forthcoming from Signature books (2020). Her creative work has appeared recently in *AGNI, Hotel Amerika, Sugar House Review, Western Humanities Review,* and *Zone 3.* She is a former managing editor of *Bellingham Review*, founding editor-in-chief of *Psaltery & Lyre*, and poetry editor for *Exponent II* magazine. She is a co-editor of *Dove Song: Heavenly Mother in Mormon Poetry* (*Peculiar Pages*, 2018).

Dovie Onice Eagar Peterson lives in Provo, Utah. She likes to wonder and sometimes write around the edges of big thinks and big feels. She loves easily. Humans, fauna, flora, culture, pretty much all creation are her fandoms. She's a mother to half a dozen beloved kiddos and spouse to a kind man.

Emily Summerhays is a Mormon heretic, born to goodly parents in the shadow of the everlasting hills; an early writer for the then-burgeoning *Feminist Mormon Housewives* blog; and a longtime resident of New York City, where she writes and strategizes in support of scientific research and education.

Esther Dale is a social work student who lives in Alaska with her family (location subject to change if she gets tired of being really cold). Her hobbies include taking photos, reading, watching *Nailed It!* on Netflix, and curating her Alaskan Malamute's Instagram account.

Rev. Dr. Fatimah S. Salleh was born in Brooklyn, NY to a Puerto-Rican and Malaysian mother and an African American father. She is the eldest of seven. Dr. Salleh received her Ph.D. in Mass Communication from the University of North Carolina at Chapel Hill. She also earned a master's degree from Syracuse University in Public Communication and a second Master's in Divinity from Duke University. She served a mission in Campinas, Brazil. She is married to Eric Sorensen and they have four children: Micah, Xavier, Ronin and Zora Grace. She is the founder of A Certain Work, an organization dedicated to educating on issues of faith, diversity, equity, and inclusion.

Gretchen Walker

Heather Harris-Bergevin accidentally writes poems at 3 a.m., but forgets them by morning or only leaves a breadcrumb trail of scratchy handwriting in her bedside notebook. Her book, *Lawless Women*, was published in 2018 with By Common Consent Press, and is available on Amazon. She usually needs a nap.

Heather Holland lives in Laramie, Wyoming where she attempts to balance motherhood, love of the outdoors, and teaching. She completed an MFA in creative writing, with a minor in gender and women's studies, at University of Wyoming. Her poetry and essays have appeared in *saltfront, The Found Poetry Review, Segullah, Exponent II, Panorama*, and in her chapbook *Mastering the Art of Joy.*

Jami Baayd is a maternal health researcher who has the great fortune of working together with women around the world to make childbirth safe and respectful. Through her travels and studies, she has been invited into some of women's most sacred spaces. Her poem honors one such place.

Jenna Colvin is a lover of reading, of writing, of meditating. She is a mother to three beautiful children and a wife to a supportive husband. She is currently pursuing a master's degree in library science with the hope that someday she will be paid to spend her time in quiet spaces surrounded by books.

Jennifer Gonzalez is a legal communicator, information designer, and immigrant and refugee rights advocate. She has a passion for storytelling in all its forms and is a strong believer in the power of narrative to change hearts, minds, and communities. She has studied human-centered design thinking and produced short documentary films exploring the human cost of legal decisions. Prior to her legal career, she was an award-winning teacher, trainer, and consultant in Washington, DC. In addition to her JD from Stanford Law School, Jennifer has an MA in Rhetoric and Composition and a BA in English from Brigham Young University.

Jennifer Perlmutter Tanner enjoys seeking God outside the box, advocating for women's issues, and community activism related to autism and immigration policy. She grew up in Central California, then earned a BA in Spanish from BYU after training to be a junior high and high school teacher. She's married to a wonderful man who practices immigration and family law; he shares her desire to help the vulnerable. She currently manages his law practice in Salt Lake City. Jennifer is a mother of four thoughtful, energetic kids who inspire her every day.

Jo Overton was raised by a strong woman, and is blessed to be wife, mother, grandmother. She is an enrolled tribal member of the Sicangu Lakota of Rosebud, and is finding her way in between two nations.

Jody England Hansen is a mixed-media artist, writer, speaker and seeker of complex wisdom. She has been a Mormon feminist, advocate, and activist for over fifty years, ever since she was a child listening in on lively fireside discussions in her parents' home during the 1960s. She recently re-matriated to Salt Lake City, where she practices learning to love people, even and especially when they disagree with her.

Judith Curtis, master gardener and long-time Desert Botanical Garden volunteer, has written poetry since she was fifty years old and has published in several journals and online sites. Her work was included in the LDS poetry anthology, *Fire in the Pasture*, and she did a tour with them. She has published two poem books for family and friends, and one called *Desert Suite,* featuring poems and photos from desert areas all over the Southwest.

Kalani Tonga is an author, educator, and mother of five, currently residing in Salt Lake City, Utah. As a member of the Feminist Mormon Housewives Board of Directors and a co-founder of FEMWOC, Kalani comes to this project with a great love of Mormon feminism in general, and a great love for Gina Colvin specifically.

Kate Kelly is an international human rights attorney and was excommunicated by the Mormon Church in 2014 for advocating for gender justice for Mormon women.

Kathryn Shields is a 28-year-old Appalachian mountain child, and a first-time poet. She is honored to be included among these remarkable religious feminists who have offered guidance and support to so many.

Katie Langston is a doubter by nature and a believer by grace. She grew up Mormon in Northern Utah, and is now a candidate for ordination in the Evangelical Lutheran Church in America. She makes her home in St. Paul, MN with her spouse and two daughters, where she works in marketing, communications, and innovation at Luther Seminary.

Katie Rasmussen is a woman, aunt, friend, and teacher who cares very much about the safety and comfort of women +. She is deeply grateful for the women + she knows who see exactly who she is and touch her pain softly.

Katy Drake Bettner is an executive in the entertainment industry. She co-founded Playful Corp with her husband, Paul, and BetRed Stories with partner, Amy Redford. Katy is active in politics and philanthropy, a member of the Women at Sundance Leadership Council, Women Donor Network, Way to Win, the TED community and serves on various boards including The Treatment Support Fund. The Bettners are active in their local wards (to the delight of some and the chagrin of others), while raising three kids (ages 10, 8, and 5) and a fluffy dog, and splitting time between McKinney TX and Sundance UT.

Kim Sandberg Turner

Kimberly Fitzpatrick Lewis is an fMh permablogger, author, public health sex educator, and critical care nurse case manager residing in CT. A twenty-four-year LDS convert member, she resigned over discrepancies of conscience in church policies pertaining to women's equality, spiritual freedom, and LGBTQ issues.

Kristen Shill, JD, is a writer and published poet. Her passion for advocacy and activism informs her career and poetry. She lives with her craft beer enthusiast spouse and feral mancub. When not enjoying the great outdoors, Kristen enjoys knitting, coffee with friends, long baths, and spicy food.

Laura Dickey is a molecular biologist, mother of two spirited daughters, Girl Scout leader, and environmental activist. She enjoys writing, teaching, and most outdoor activities. She does not enjoy battling household entropy.

Laura Lawrence is an environmental scientist who lives in the San Francisco Bay Area.

Laurie Burk has been involved in the online Mormon feminist community since 2004 when she started blogging under the name "Not Ophelia" at *Feminist Mormon Housewives*. She and her husband, Dan, have a home in Southern California where they live when they are not living abroad. They are the parents of one daughter.

Laurie A. Shipp's ancestors first joined the church in Kirtland, OH and came west to Utah with the Saints in 1847. Prior to 2013, she was a lifelong active member who served in many callings on both the ward and stake level, including early morning seminary teacher. She moved back to Utah recently after a difficult faith transition that ended in divorce.

While she's no longer an active member, she still honors her Mormon heritage and those ancestors who came before her. She has six children and eight grandchildren.

Lesley Butterfield Harrop is a nurse by trade with a love for writing. She believes in the healing power of words. Lesley has written a number of articles for various online publications, but she is new to composing poetry.

Lindsay Denton lives in Las Vegas, Nevada with her husband and three children. She is a writer, a foodie, and a speech pathologist, and she enjoys gardening, cooking, and listening to audiobooks. Her essays have been featured on *Segullah* and in *Exponent II* magazine, and she blogs at the-exponent.com.

Lindsay Hansen Park is the executive director of the Sunstone Education Foundation and the host of the *Year of Polygamy* podcast.

Lisa Butterworth is a Licensed Professional Counselor and founder of Feminist Mormon Housewives.

Lismarie Ellis Nyland grew up in San Diego County in the Mormon faith and tradition. She continued as a faithful member of the Church of Jesus Christ of Latter-day Saints until 2012, when she was thrust into a massive faith crisis and later transitioned out of activity in the church. She is a photographer, piano teacher, substitute school teacher, mother of four, and wife to one.

Maggie Hurst is a creative soul, mother, partner and lover of words. Born of bold and imaginative pioneer ancestry, she feels deeply connected to her lineage and the heritage of stories that she carries. She believes we are all intricately connected through the stories of our own pioneering efforts in this wild world. When she's not crafting words, she can often be found creating anew in various mediums of vibrant textures and colors or settling in to discover the art of others.

Malena Crockett is a novelist, a poet, a memoirist, and a sixth-generation descendant of Mormon pioneer immigrants, emigrants, and migrants. She keeps one finger on the pulse of contemporary Mormonism, and writes of her own and her ancestors' experiences as participants in the evolution of nearly two centuries of Mormon faith and community. Malena hosts the Facebook pages "Women Going Woke"

and "Molly Mormon Goes Rogue." Her web site is
www.malenacrockett.com.

Mandy L. Lyons enjoys walking about with the dogs in the wonder, dust, shrubs, and brambles of the outdoors, with the occasional insect or small critter along to provide entertainment. Her other great joy resides in intense, unrestricted discussions which creep into the wee hours of morning. After work, either of these intermingles with her numerous hobbies. She cares immensely about family and community. She has been herself for forty-three years and expects more of that in the future.

Margaret Olsen Hemming is the Editor in Chief for *Exponent II*, a magazine that has been publishing the voices of Mormon women since 1974.

Marie Murphy is a writer and adventurer. She brings her experiences from growing up around the world, the unexpected lessons she learned as a classroom teacher, and her time in the corporate world into her writing. Her work is often tied to her religious upbringing and deep-seated spirituality. When not writing or adventuring, you can find Marie walking her dog, cheering on her local soccer team (Real Salt Lake), or trying a new recipe.

Marilyn Bushman-Carlton has written three poetry books, a children's poetry book, and a biography. She has won awards from the Association of Mormon Letters, the Comstock Review, and the Utah Arts Council. Her poems have appeared in numerous journals and anthologies, including *Fire in the Pasture,* and *Discoveries: Two Centuries of Poems by Mormon Women.* An essay appeared in *Baring Witness: 36 Mormon Women Talk Candidly about Love, Sex, and Marriage.* She and her husband, Blaine, enjoy traveling and spending time with their five children and sixteen grandchildren. The two of them live in Sun Crest, above Draper, Utah.

Maxine Hanks is a theologian whose work explores gender in LDS tradition and Christianity. She also serves in LDS and interfaith ministry. She was a visiting fellow at Harvard Divinity School and a research fellow with Utah Humanities Council. Her first book, *Women and Authority,* recovered LDS women's history and theology, while subsequent books treat LDS or Utah history. Her essays, articles, and poetry appear in books, anthologies, and journals. She did her bachelor's in gender studies with history, and graduate work in history, gender and religious studies. She has lectured in gender studies at the University of Utah, and guest lectured at several schools. She has also presented often on gender, history, and religion.

Melody Newey Johnson believes in love. Her poems have appeared in *Exponent II, Segullah, Irreantum*, and in numerous anthologies and online literary journals. In addition, her poetry has been featured in the collaborative art exhibit, *Ceremonies of Innocence: The Girls Are Now Women*, at the Salt Lake Art Center. She currently serves with her husband in their local LDS ward teaching Sunbeams in Primary. She lives and works as a nurse in Salt Lake City.

Melonie Cannon is called many things: Mom, Wife, Writer, Healer, Teacher, Guide, and Friend. She explores these experiences through her writing and podcast on *Segullah* where she has been a staff member since 2006. You can find her leading guided meditations, reading, drumming, playing sound bowls, or playing a good old round of Monopoly with her four wonderful kids. She currently lives near the mountains in Utah.

Mette Harrison is an essay writer, a novelist, a nationally ranked triathlete, a Princeton PhD, and, apparently, a poet.

Mindy May Farmer is a recent graduate of the SNHU master's program in English, fulfilling a life-long educational goal. She is a freelance writer, blogger, and mom of four who is now pursuing a new career as an adjunct instructor of English. Her interests include discovering new authors, writing about her life, and traveling to new places. Mindy hopes to return to London one day and to discover the world through her travels.

Mindy Gledhill is an award-winning indie singer songwriter whose work has been featured on prime-time television shows (*Bones, The Good Wife, So You Think You Can Dance,* and *Dancing with the Stars,* to name a few). Additionally, her songs have been used in major television ad campaigns (Fruit of the Loom's 2012 Olympic ad campaign, AAA Insurance's 2014 Super Bowl ad campaign, LG Phones, Reliant Power). She has toured in the United States and Japan. Her latest album *Rabbit Hole* released on January 25, 2019.

Moana Uluave Hafoka was born in Salt Lake City, Utah. Moana is a Gates Millennium Scholar and graduated with University Honors from Brigham Young University in English and a minor in sociology. In May 2014, she graduated with a master's degree from the Harvard Graduate School of Education. She previously served as a community program assistant at the Sorenson Unity Center, as a teaching assistant with the Boston University Prison Education program, and as a paraprofessional at Edison Elementary School. Moana lives in Glendale with her husband, Maika, and their baby, Linita.

Morgen Willis used to be a little girl with a microphone, who loved her bicycle. Now she's a woman with a family, a laptop, and a ukulele, who dreams of travelling to beautiful, interesting places. She's currently living the Toddler Mom life in Boston.

Nancy Ross is a faculty member in the Interdisciplinary Arts and Sciences Department at Dixie State University, where she has been teaching for twelve years. Her degrees are in art history, but she moonlights as a sociologist of religion. She recently co-edited a book with Sara K.S. Hanks titled *Where We Must Stand: Ten Years of Feminist Mormon Housewives.*

Natasha Helfer Parker, LCMFT, CST has been in practice as a mental health professional for over twenty years, primarily working with issues of relational health, faith transitions and journeys, and sexuality. She writes a blog called *The Mormon Therapist* and hosts the podcasts *Mormon Mental Health* and *Mormon Sex Info*. She also produces *Sex Talk with Natasha.*

Nicole Thomas Durrant is an attorney specializing in immigration. She lives on the California central coast with her husband and kids.

Olea Plum was born to two returned missionaries in rural Australia and has participated in the church on three continents. Now living in Germany with her husband of one year, she still calls herself a Mormon. Always in love with words and an advocate for justice, Olea is a blogger at *The Exponent II* and has contributed to *Segullah*. She is currently piecing her third quilt and designing her fourth. This is her first published poem.

Olivia Meikle is producer and co-host of the *What'sHerName* women's history podcast, author of *Around the World in 80 Diapers*, mother to three gloriously-feminist teenage sons, wife to one impossibly-perfect husband, and she teaches English and women's and gender studies at Naropa University. She lives in Boulder, Colorado.

Page Turner is a native of Roanoke, Virginia. She collects items of deep personal meaning to painstakingly create delicate objects that honor the feminine along with the desires, experiences and roles of women. Her powerful assemblages include found objects such as fur, wood, shells, paper, and bone that firmly position her work culturally and geographically in the Appalachian region. Paige stitches these objects together with family heirlooms, antique fabric, and other personal objects, by hand, to create delicate sculptural pieces infused with a new feminist aesthetic and a soulful reverence for her heritage.

Rachel Farmer is a Brooklyn-based artist, originally from Provo, Utah. She works in a variety of media, including hand-built ceramic sculpture, photography and video. Her work has been exhibited nationally, and is included in the *Brooklyn Museum's Feminist Art Base*, a digital archive. She was awarded a 2013-14 A.I.R. Gallery Fellowship, and was a resident artist at the Museum of Arts and Design in 2016. Recent work includes a site-specific installation for the Leslie-Lohman Museum of Gay & Lesbian Art in NYC (2017), and a solo exhibition at Granary Arts in Ephraim, UT (2018). For more info, visit *rachelfarmer.com*.

Rachel Hunt Steenblik is a Mormon feminist theologian and poet. She won the 2017 Association for Mormon Letters poetry award for her book, *Mother's Milk: Poems in Search of Heavenly Mother*, published by BCC Press and has another volume, *I Gave Her a Name*, set for release in 2019. She co-edited Oxford University Press's *Mormon Feminism: Essential Writings,* alongside Joanna Brooks and Hannah Wheelwright. Hunt Steenblik finished her PhD coursework in philosophy of religion and theology at Claremont Graduate University, and has a BA in philosophy from Brigham Young University, and an MS in library and information science from Simmons College.

Raini Hamilton is an aspiring writer and avid reader. She holds a bachelor's degree in social work and enjoys meeting new people. She loves camping in the mountains with her husband and their three children. She is proud to call both Idaho and Montana home.

Rebecca de Schweinitz is an associate professor of history at Brigham Young University, where she has taught since 2006. She received her PhD from the University of Virginia, has been a fellow at Yale's Gilder Lehrman Center, and is the author of *If We Could Change the World: Young People and America's Long Struggle for Racial Equality* (Chapel Hill: University of North Carolina Press, 2009). Rebecca has authored various articles on youth in American history, including work on Mormon youth. She also currently serves on the Board of Directors for *Dialogue: A Journal of Mormon Thought*.

Reija Rawle is a physician and mother to three curly-and-red-headed children. The first poem she loved is "How Mrs. Santa Claus Saved Christmas" by Phyllis McGinley, which her parents read from a treasured, carefully preserved photocopy of the 1961 *Family Circle* magazine. She started reading poetry more regularly after finding and using "Woman" by Nikki Giovanni in her 12th grade *Norton Anthology* textbook during an argument with a male classmate. Her favorite poem in medical school was "From Blossoms" by Li-Young Lee, and her favorite poems as a mother are all by Ashley Mae Hoiland.

RevaBeth Russell is a feminist, Mormon, teacher, mother, learner, and creator. Not necessarily in that order.

Sally Peel is a friendly woman who loves her family and community.

Sara Burlingame was adopted into a tribe of Mormon feminists in 2006, via Feminist Mormon Housewives. She has never looked back.

Sara Hughes-Zabawa is a licensed clinical social worker and is passionate about helping clients to achieve better balance and learn to thrive as they enhance the quality of their lives. Sara partners with clients to help foster the bravery and skills necessary to support holistic wellness that honors their mind-body-spirit connection. Sara received a Master of Social Work with an emphasis in mental health and interpersonal practice, communities and social systems, with a minor in community organizing, and a graduate certificate in women's studies from the University of Michigan.

Sara Katherine Staheli Hanks is a writer, editorial assistant, tarot enthusiast, and mother of two from Utah. She is the co-editor of *Where We Must Stand: Ten Years of Feminist Mormon Housewives* (2018), a collection of blog posts written by Mormon feminists.

Susan Elizabeth Howe is a poet and retired professor living in Ephraim, Utah, with her husband, Cless Young.

Susan Krueger-Barber is a performance and installation artist who occupies alter-egos to inflate, expand, and pop tension inherent in discussions of gender fluidity, urban planning, and the status quo. The audience's attention is aimed to theatrically induce pursuits involving the expansion of limited political frameworks while utilizing empathic theory and erratically constructed installations that borrow their meaning from origin stories of her respective lineages, namely DIY, feminist, and

Mormon. Krueger-Barber ignites action by fueling memory, connection, and self-reflection in atmospheres that create safe spaces and an undeniably energized mode of seeing that results in laughter, tears, and a common humility.

Tamra Wright is a creative artist of anything related to design. She received her BA from BYU in 1981 in the department of Art and Design. Her cap and gown pictures included a 6-week-old daughter in a blessing dress. Her degree led her to a career in kitchen and bath design for 20+ years. She completed a master's program in textile and pattern design in 2014 from the California School of Professional Fabric Design in Berkeley, California. She continues to work on a children's book called *Paisley's Planet*, and she is currently starting a new career as a post-partum doula.

Taylor Carver Kevan has a BA in advertising with an emphasis in copywriting from Brigham Young University. She is a bisexual Mormon woman learning how to thrive with anxiety. (Thank you, therapy and medication!) She lives in Portland, Oregon with her husband and son.

Tresa Edmunds is a writer, artist, and activist. Her work has appeared in the *Guardian UK*, *Better Homes and Gardens*, and from one end of the internet to another. She is also the CEO and co-founder of HavenTree, a subscription box and online shop specializing in self-care.

Twila Newey has an MFA from The Jack Kerouac School of Disembodied Poetics at Naropa University. She lives and writes near San Francisco, California.

Wendy H. Christian is a psychoanalyst and licensed clinical social worker in New York City. Prior to becoming a mental health professional, she studied American literature at BYU, where she did a rhetorical and narrative analysis of women in the Book of Mormon. Her master's thesis is titled *And Well She Can Persuade: The Power and Presence of Women in the Book of Mormon*. Wendy obtained a second master's degree in clinical social work at Fordham University, and did extensive post-graduate training in psychoanalysis and religion, and in marriage and family therapy, at the Blanton-Peale Institute. Wendy is a proud Mormon feminist, blogs at *Exponent II*, and has a private practice in Manhattan. She can be contacted through her web site, *wendychristiantherapy.com*.

Gina Colvin is currently a divinity school student at Laidlaw College in New Zealand, having chucked in the towel as a lecturer in education to pursue her call to ministry! However, she is still on staff at University of Canterbury as an adjunct research fellow. Gina is a discourse analyst, auto ethnographer, narrative inquirer, cultural studies, and media analyst, and a post-colonial, indigenous decolonizer by methodology.
She enjoys trying to upend taken-for-granted ideas, and burning ideologies that sustain unequal power relations to the ground – particularly in religious contexts. She likes to think she's a post-colonial pyrotheologist (thanks, Peter Rollins). She hosts a podcast (*A Thoughtful Faith*), and a blog (*Kiwi Mormon*), and she is a retreat host.

A Word from Our Sponsor ~

Thank you for reading *We Hold Your Name*. If you have found it helpful or inspiring, we would be grateful for a positive review on Amazon.com or Goodreads or any of your favorite book review outlets. Proceeds from this publication will go toward helping emerging feminist writers and artists, especially women of color, to find their place in the creative human universe.

If you would like to know more about Feminist Mormon Housewives, please look for us online at
https://www.feministmormonhousewives.org/
and on Facebook at https://m.me/FeministMormonHousewives/

Other works by Feminist Mormon Housewives:

Where We Must Stand: Ten Years of Feminist Mormon Housewives, Sara K.S. Hanks and Nancy Ross (2018).